Writing

Developmental Continuum

The Writing Developmental Continuum was researched, developed and written by Glenda Raison, Education Department of Western Australia, in collaboration with Judith Rivalland, Edith Cowan University.

First Steps was developed by the Education Department of Western Australia under the direction of Alison Dewsbury.

STEPS Professional Development & Consulting
Salem, MA

STEPS Professional Development & Consulting
97 Boston Street
Salem, MA 01970
A division of Edith Cowan University Resources for Learning
Offices throughout the world

First published 1994 by Addison Wesley Longman
Previously published 1996 by Heinemann, USA
Currently published 2004 *STEPS* Professional Development & Consulting
on behalf of the Education Department of Western Australia

Library of Congress Cataloging-in-Publication Data
CIP is on file with the Library of Congress

ISBN 0-9746654-2-8
First Steps Writing Developmental Continuum

Contents

Part I

Foundations of First Steps

In this section the philosophical and theoretical framework of First Steps is set out. Specific points are made about the teaching of children for whom English is a second language and some suggestions are made about factors which foster effective learning in the classroom.

Foundations of First Steps includes:

- Linking Assessment to Teaching
    The Developmental Continua
    Teaching Strategies
    Underlying Theoretical Assumptions
    Important Considerations
    Teaching Children for whom English is a Second Language

- Effective Learning
    Problem Solving
    Embeddedness
    Working Memory
    Interaction
    Time

- 'The Three Rs'
    Reflecting
    Representing
    Reporting

Linking Assessment to Teaching

In an increasingly complex world, re-evaluating methods of teaching and learning is important. At the same time, methods of evaluating development, especially in relation to testing, have become highly problematic. Effective teachers have always used systematic observation and recording as a means of assessment. The First Steps materials have been developed to give teachers an explicit way of mapping children's progress through observation. The Developmental Continua validate what teachers know about children.

The Developmental Continua

The continua have been developed to provide teachers with a way of looking at what children can actually do and how they can do it, in order to inform planning for further development. It is recognised that language learning is holistic and develops in relation to the context in which it is used. However, given the complexity of each mode of language, a continuum has been provided for reading, writing, spelling and oral language, in order to provide teachers with in-depth information in each one of these areas.

The Continua make explicit some of the indicators, or descriptors of behaviour, that will help teachers identify how children are constructing and communicating meaning through language. The indicators were extracted from research into the development of literacy in English-speaking children. It was found that indicators tend to cluster together, i.e. if children exhibit one behaviour they tend to exhibit several other related behaviours. Each cluster of indicators was arbitrarily called a 'phase'. This clustering of indicators into phases allows teachers to map overall progress while demonstrating that children's

language does not develop in a linear sequence. The concept of a phase was shown to be valid by the Australian Council for Educational Research in their initial research into the validity of the *Writing: Developmental Continuum*.

Individual children may exhibit a range of indicators from various phases at any one time. 'Key' indicators are used to place children within a specific phase, so that links can be made to appropriate learning experiences. Key indicators describe behaviours that are typical of a phase. Developmental records show that children seldom progress in a neat and well-sequenced manner; instead they may remain in one phase for some length of time and move rapidly through other phases. Each child is a unique individual with different life experiences so that no two developmental pathways are the same.

The indicators are not designed to provide evaluative criteria through which every child is expected to progress in sequential order. They reflect a developmental view of teaching and learning and are clearly related to the contexts in which development is taking place. That is, language development is not seen as a 'naturalistic' or universal phenomena through which all children progress in the same way. Children's achievements, however, provide evidence of an overall pattern of development which accommodates a wide range of individual difference.

Teaching Strategies

The other major purpose of these documents is to link phases of development to teaching strategies, in order to help teachers make decisions about appropriate practice in the light of children's development. It is important that within this framework teachers value individual difference and cultural diversity. **It is not intended that these** strategies are prescriptive; they offer a range of practices from which teachers might select, depending upon the purposes of any particular language program and the needs of the children in their class. The purpose of the Continua is to link assessment with teaching and learning in a way that will support children and provide practical assistance for teachers.

Underlying Theoretical Assumptions

The First Steps indicators and suggested activities have been based on the following theoretical assumptions:

- Language learning takes place through interactions in meaningful events, rather than through isolated language activities
- Language learning is seen as holistic; that is, each mode of language supports and enhances overall language development
- Language develops in relation to the context in which it is used; that is, it develops according to the situation, the topic under discussion, and the relationship between the participants
- Language develops through the active engagement of the learners
- Language develops through interaction and the joint construction of meaning in a range of contexts
- Language learning can be enhanced by learners monitoring their own progress
- The way in which children begin to make sense of the world is constructed through the language they use and reflects cultural understandings and values

It is important that the indicators and activities are interpreted from the perspective of these underlying assumptions about language learning.

Important Considerations

The First Steps materials have been designed to help teachers map children's progress and suggest strategies for further development. When making decisions about what to do next, there are a number of issues that need to be considered.

Teachers' actions, strategies and ways of interacting with children reflect particular values and assumptions about learning. Through these interactions, children construct a view of what 'counts' as literacy in a particular classroom setting. This is manifested in the way:

a) teachers make decisions about selecting materials and texts
b) activities are carried out using the materials and texts
c) teachers talk with children
d) children talk with each other
e) what gets talked about (topic)

The decisions made by teachers play a role in how children come to understand what counts as literacy. In some cases there may be major conflicting and competing value systems at work leading to a variety of outcomes.

For example, the text Cinderella implicitly constructs a particular view of the world which presents women in a stereotypical role, not necessarily reflecting the role of women in modern society.

Clearly the text can be used in a number of different ways. It might be used as a shared book experience in which the teacher engages the children in a reading of the text, developing talk around the concepts of print and the repeated patterns of the text. In focusing on these aspects, the teacher would be constructing a view of reading which places emphasis on print rather than the message and leaves the role of women, as presented in the text, unchallenged. However, if the teacher encouraged the children to talk about the text in a way that challenged this view, through talking about their own experience of women and presenting other literature, the teacher would begin the process of helping children to detect the values within text.

Moving from this activity to asking the children to draw a picture of their own siblings and write a description about them, the teacher's response will signal to children what is important. Focusing on spelling and grammar will indicate that correctness is valued above content, whereas focusing on the content by discussing the characteristics of their siblings and comparing these with the ugly sisters, enables the children to become 'critical' readers.

The teaching strategies that are used and the texts selected are very powerful transmitters of cultural knowledge and how children construct the task of learning to be literate. In relation to the texts selected, what seems to be critical is the way in which they are used, rather than merely trying to select the 'right' text, because all texts convey values of some sort.

Given that literacy learning is such a complex task, teachers will use a range of different strategies for different purposes according to the needs of the children. However, what seems to be important is that teachers are consciously aware of which strategies they are selecting, why, and how these actions will impact on the children's understanding of what counts as literacy.

Another aspect of decision making is related to recognition of the specific skills, attitudes and knowledge children bring to the classroom. In order to enable children to feel confident in their own abilities, it is important to recognise, value, consolidate and extend the diversity of children's competence through classroom practice.

When planning a language program which will put the suggested strategies from First Steps into practice, based on the knowledge gained through mapping the children's progress through the indicators, it may be useful to consider the following:

– What new ways of using and understanding language do you want children to develop?
– What sort of contexts will enable this development to occur?
– What sort of texts (oral, written, media, dramatic) will facilitate this learning?
– How will children need to be supported in processing these texts?

– What new skills, processing and knowledge might the children need explicit understanding of in order to complete the language task?
– What underlying values and assumptions encompass your literacy program?
– How will the interactions between you and the children facilitate your aims for literacy development?
– How can you help children to monitor their own progress?

Caroline Barratt-Pugh
Judith Rivalland

Teaching Children for whom English is a Second Language

(or children whose language of home differs from that of the teacher)

When teaching children for whom English is a second language it is important to recognise:

• the diversity and richness of experience and expertise that children bring to school

• cultural values and practices that may be different from those of the teacher

• that children need to have the freedom to use their own languages and to code-switch when necessary

• that the context and purpose of each activity needs to make sense to the learner

• that learning needs to be supported through talk and collaborative peer interaction

• that the child may need a range of 'scaffolds' to support learning and that the degree of support needed will vary over time, context and degree of content complexity

• that children will need time and support so that they do not feel pressured

- that supportive attitudes of peers may need to be actively fostered
- that it may be difficult to assess children's real achievements and that the active involvement of parents will make a great deal of difference, as will on-going monitoring.

Action Research in a wide range of classrooms over a four-year period indicates that effective teaching strategies for children for whom English is a second language and children whose language of home differs from that of the teacher are:

- Modelling
- Sharing
- Joint Construction of Meaning
- The provision of Scaffolds or Frameworks
- Involvement of children in self-monitoring of their achievements
- Open Questions

    Open Questions that are part of sharing or joint construction of meaning, e.g. questions such as 'Do you think we should do ... or ... to make it work?' or 'It was very clever to do that. How did you think of it?', are very helpful. When children are asked closed questions to which teachers already know the answers, such as 'What colour/shape/size is it?', children often feel threatened and tend to withdraw.

These factors are expanded in the 'Supporting Diversity' chapters in First Steps *Reading: Resource Book* and *Oral Language: Resource Book*.

Caroline Barratt-Pugh
Anna Sinclair

Effective Learning: PEWIT

Many factors enhance or inhibit learning. The following factors help children and adults learn effectively. They are reflected in the First Steps Developmental Continua and Resource Books and underpin all the teaching and learning activities.

- Problem-solving
- Embeddedness
- Working memory
- Interaction
- Time

Problem Solving

Effective learning occurs when children and adults are able to modify and extend their understandings in order to make sense of a situation which has challenged them. This is the essence of problem solving. Effective problem solvers are those who can:
- identify a specific concept or skill as one that is posing a problem
- decide to do something about it
- have a go at finding a solution, using a range of strategies
- keep going until they are satisfied that their new understandings or skills provide the solution they have been reaching for.

Children

Children are natural learners. Young children are constantly learning about their environment through interaction, exploration, trial and error and through 'having a go' at things. As a child's world of experience expands, so deeper understandings are constructed. Additional learning is always built upon existing foundations, and existing structures are constantly being adapted to accommodate fresh insights. Children use language to make sense of their world, imposing order on it and endeavouring to control it.

In coming to terms with the spoken and written language:
- (i) children need to see clearly the purposes for talking and listening, reading and writing so that they can adopt goals for themselves
- (ii) children are engaged in problem solving when they explore oral and written language in their environment, in play and in role-play
- (iii) children are problem solving when they attempt to represent the written language on paper
- (iv) children are problem solving when they attempt to represent oral language in print

Teachers

Teachers are faced with a multitude of challenges every day. How can a difficult concept be introduced? How can the classroom be constantly stimulating for children without risking teacher burn-out? How can a different management strategy be implemented without risk of losing control? How can new insights into gender equity be incorporated into the curriculum?

In implementing change, it is helpful if each challenge can be represented as a problem which can be solved using the technique of 'having a go'; trying out a strategy; reflecting on the result; and then having another go, having slightly modified the strategy, Teachers sometimes expect too much of themselves. They should not expect things to work perfectly first time round. The essence of problem-solving is that strategies and understandings are gradually refined over time. There is seldom one right or easy answer, but a whole range of solutions on a variety of levels that fit the children's needs, teachers' own personal styles and the demands of the tasks.

Embeddedness (Contextualisation)

Most people have had the experience of listening to a speaker and being totally unable to make sense of what is being said. In such circumstances one is apt to say 'I switched off. It didn't make a word of sense.' People need to be able to make connections between their own current understandings and new learning that is being undertaken. A person who knows nothing of mechanics may be quite unable to follow a lecture on car maintenance, but may be able to work things out if the car is there with the bonnet up and the parts clearly visible.

If the context and the problem are embedded in reality and make sense to the learner, then the learner can engage in productive problem solving. If the problem is not embedded in, and seen to be arising from, past experience, then rote learning may occur, but real learning, which is capable of generalisation, will probably not take place.

Children

Children learn effectively in contexts that make sense to them. The challenges which children face and the problems which they attack in their early environment are embedded in familiar, real life contexts. This can be seen quite clearly in early oral language development, when language acquisition is closely tied to the immediate environment and to current needs.

In coming to terms with written language:

(i)   children need to be given opportunities to interact with print (read and write) in contexts which make sense to them and which have their counterpart in the real world, in role play and in real situations, e.g. making shopping lists, identifying stop signs

(ii) children need to see adults explicitly modelling reading and writing for a variety of purposes in real situations, e.g. reading and writing notes

(iii) children need to interact not only with books, but with the wide range of print found in daily life, e.g. in newspapers and environmental print.

Teachers

Teachers also need to start from where they are, working within their own familiar context. The First Steps resources offer a number of alternative ways of looking at teaching and a great many strategies and activities which people have found to be useful. Once teachers have decided what problem they want to solve or what challenge they wish to take on, they need to start from a context which makes sense to them and gradually incorporate alternative strategies within their own repertoires. The new learning needs to be embedded within the context of the old and teaching strategies need to be slowly adapted to meet new challenges and different understandings.

Working Memory (Mental Space)

Working memory, which is sometimes called M-space, is very different from long or short term memory. It is, in effect, a measure of the number of discrete elements which the mind can cope with at any one time. A good analogy is that of the juggler, who can juggle competently with four or five balls, but when given one too many, will drop the lot.

Once ideas and skills become familiar as a result of practice over a period of time, two things happen. One is that the learner does not have to think consciously about how to do them any more, so much less space is taken up in the working memory, e.g. spelling a very familiar word. The other is that several different skills gradually become one skill. For example when learning to print children have to manipulate the pencil, remember the formation of letters and consider the order in which the marks have to appear on the page. With practice these individual skills will integrate to become one skill.

Any emotional issue or concern will 'fill up' the mental space more quickly than anything else. Fear, anger or worry may totally inhibit a person's capacity to learn. Most people have had the experience of being unable to concentrate because their mind is fully taken up by an all-consuming emotion. The only thing to do is to give oneself time to 'get it together' again. In the meantime performance on any task will be poor and will continue to deteriorate until the cloud of emotion has lifted. If people say 'I just couldn't think straight', they are usually speaking the truth.

Children

Children focus their entire attention on one element which they perceive to be a challenge. Young children can only cope with one or two different factors at once. As they get older they can juggle with an increasing number of elements, although there is a limit to the amount that anyone can handle.

In coming to terms with the written language:

(i) children may only be able to focus on one or two different factors at any one time. For example, during a shared reading lesson one child may focus on the meaning and spelling of an unusual word in a story, whereas another may be emotionally involved with the characters. Neither may have 'heard' the teacher explaining the use of speech marks.

(ii) as they focus on one skill children may temporarily lose competence in another very familiar skill. For example when a child is absorbed in getting ideas onto paper the quality of handwriting may deteriorate.

(iii) children need to practise and apply a particular aspect of language in a number of contexts until it becomes automatic. Opportunities to practise in stimulating circumstances constitute an important component of all language programs, so that 'mental space' is made available for more complex learning.

(iv) children may appear to make significant regressions if their 'mental space' is fully taken up with an emotional issue relating to home or school.

Teachers

Teachers sometimes make impossible demands on themselves. They are also only able to cope with a certain number of new things at any one time. Instead of attempting everything at once, they need to try one small component of a task first and then build on that. For instance, it is impossible to attempt to observe all the children in a class at once. The secret is to focus on only three or four children a week, looking only at the key indicators. Children thought to be at risk can gradually be placed on the continuum, looking at all indicators.

It is important not to try to do too much at once. If circumstances become overwhelming for any reason, such as trouble at home, too many extraneous duties or ill health, teachers should wait for things to calm down before trying anything new.

Interaction

Interaction is of fundamental importance to human beings. People need to discuss ideas, build on each other's expertise, use each other as sounding boards and work creatively as communities of learners. It is through talk that ideas are generated, refined and extended.

Children

Children need unlimited opportunities to interact with adults and with other children in their daily lives. They need to interact with others to plan, explore, problem-solve, question, discuss and direct their activities. In doing so they try out and modify their ideas. As they use language in social situations they refine their language use and learn more about how language works.

In coming to terms with the written language:

(i) children need freedom to interact with adults in discussions about writing and reading. These discussions should not always be dominated by adults. Children need opportunities to direct conversation. The adult role may be to provide feedback and reinforcement.

(ii) children need freedom to interact with their peers to discuss problems and to formulate and clarify their ideas as they write

(iii) children need to feel safe to ask for help when they need it.

(iv) children need freedom to experiment with written language in socially supportive situations.

Teachers

Teachers also need time and opportunities to interact with their colleagues. Often the most profitable interactions take place informally between staff members who trust and respect each other. Time can also be put aside at a regular meeting for a school staff to discuss and share professional issues and insights regarding the implementation of First Steps or interesting new initiatives being undertaken by different teachers. One school developed a sharing strategy whereby every staff member concentrated on one specific strategy for a week or two, after which all reported back. This school took advantage of the wealth of expertise which is to be found in any staff room.

It is also extremely helpful to interact with parents informally as well as in more formal conferences to share insights about the children. Interacting with children is also of crucial importance, encouraging a two-way process which will enrich both teacher and child as each listens and responds to the other. Conferences between teacher, parent and child as co-members of the community of learners can also be very profitable.

Time

Children

In their everyday lives children have time to construct understandings gradually through inquiry, exploration and problem solving. They also have time to consolidate and integrate these understandings through practice. The amount of time needed to practise new skills and learnings will vary from child to child. Some may need to apply these understandings in only a few situations before they come to terms with them. Others will need to apply the understandings more frequently and in a wider variety of situations before they can begin to generalise and transfer them.

In coming to terms with the written language:

(i) children need opportunities to have regular and on-going involvement in strategies such as shared book experiences, language experience and playing with language, in order to foster their understandings about how the written language works

(ii) children need opportunities to have regular involvement in activities which give them independent practice in their own time, at their own pace, as often as is needed in both reading and writing

Teachers

Teachers need to be as kind to themselves as they are to their children. They need to give themselves time for reflection; time for experimentation and having a go; time to refine and develop strategies already in place; time for sharing with colleagues and parents and time to enjoy their job. Every adult is growing and developing throughout life. Real growth takes time in every sphere of life and development can be enhanced but not hurried. Teachers need to be confident that they are comfortable with the strategies they are implementing and time will be on their side.

Effective Learning: 'The Three Rs'

Adults and children are all learners moving along a continuum. Teachers and children come together as a community of learners. All can benefit from the three Rs:

- Reflecting
- Representing
- Reporting

Reflecting

Children

Children need time to reflect on an experience and on what they have learned from it. Too often they hustle from one learning activity to another, with no time, no space and no structure to help them stand back and think about what they have learned. If they are encouraged to pause and reflect on the insights they have gained and on things that have suddenly started to make sense to them, they will consciously take control of their learning in a new way. They will develop an awareness of specific understandings and the place of those understandings in the overall scheme of things. They will come to value and respect themselves as learners and will become aware of their own learning processes.

Teachers

Teachers need to take time to reflect on their teaching practice. They need to congratulate themselves on their many successes, to consider their goals and take stock of their current situation. Studies have shown, for instance, that almost all primary school teachers firmly believe in developmental learning, but this is not always reflected in their approach to teaching. Teachers may reflect on their teaching practice by asking themselves questions such as: Are my beliefs and theoretical understandings reflected in my current classroom practice? Are the needs of all children being met? Are children engaged in active learning? Are they interacting effectively with others?

It is always worth taking time to reflect on the reality of daily classroom experience, to analyse strengths and to pin-point the areas that may need extra attention. Management strategies, interaction with parents, collaborative work with other staff members and teacher's own professional development are all areas which can provide food for thought from time to time.

Representing

Children

Children may need to represent their learning in a very concrete form. This may be by drawing a picture, constructing a diagram or by writing down their thoughts. In some learning areas such as maths or science it may involve constructing a model.

Teachers

Teachers may need to clarify their reflections by listing one or two items that seem to be significant. Even if no action is taken immediately, an insight will have been captured and recorded for future use. If an idea is written down it is likely to become a reality.

Reporting

Children

Children need to clarify their understandings by talking about them. Children refine, consolidate and extend their learning by reporting on what they know to a peer, a small group or their teacher. This type of reporting occurs best in a natural context when a child is not under any stress and does not feel 'on show.'

Teachers

Teachers may wish to contribute to the process of school planning by reporting on what they consider to be essential goals, strategies and issues for their schools and their students. Every staff member has a crucial contribution to make which will enrich and extend the operations of the school community. Too often the richness and depth of a teacher's experience is confined to one classroom instead of being available for all members of the educational community. All teachers need the support of every other teacher if children are to gain the full benefit of growing up in a community of learners.

Part II

About Writing

This section provides some general information about writing in the First Steps program.

'About Writing' includes:

- **Effective Communication**
- **What Do We Know About Writing?**
  Principles of Writing
  Differences Between Oral and Written Language
- **How to Use the Writing Developmental Continuum**
  Predict
  Collect Data
  Involve parents and children
  Link Assessment with Teaching
  Monitor Progress

The post lady is collecting
the letters.
She is wearing a uniform.

EFFECTIVE COMMUNICATION

EFFECTIVE COMMUNICATION can be achieved by focusing on activities based on purposeful language interactions. Purposeful talk is one of the major means through which children construct and refine their understandings of language. Talk should underpin all language activities.

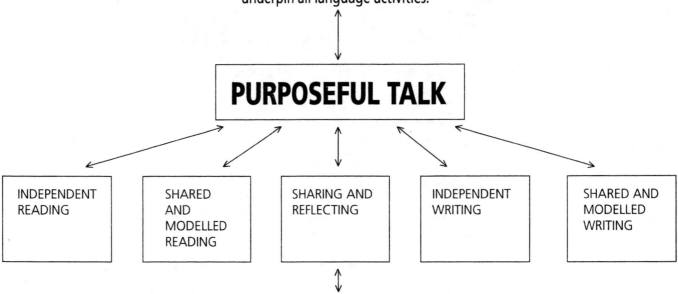

PURPOSEFUL TALK

- INDEPENDENT READING
- SHARED AND MODELLED READING
- SHARING AND REFLECTING
- INDEPENDENT WRITING
- SHARED AND MODELLED WRITING

PURPOSEFUL TALK

Communication occurs when the speaker has effectively relayed his/her meaning to the listener.

Provide opportunities for:
- discussion across the curriculum;
- negotiation;
- group interaction;
- brainstorming;
- clarification of values and issues;
- reflective response to own and others' contributions;
- reading and retelling;
- storytelling;
- news telling;
- drama;
- reporting;
- debating and arguing;
- questioning and enquiring.

PURPOSEFUL WRITING

Communication occurs when the writer has effectively relayed his/her meaning to the reader.
Good spelling is a factor in effectively relaying meaning.

Provide opportunities for:
- learning about writing;
- learning through writing;
- analysing different forms in written context;
- modelled writing;
- editing;
- writing for different purposes and audiences; and
- self evaluation of writing development.

Encourage children to develop spelling skills through:
- word study activities, e.g. derivations, origins, morphemic units;
- visual patterning activities;
- identifying critical features of words;
- using spelling resources;
- word sorting;
- use of personal lists;
- proof reading;
- a range of strategies.

PURPOSEFUL READING

Effective communication occurs when a reader creates, interprets and analyses meanings from text.

Provide opportunities for:
- reading for a wide range of purposes;
- reading a wide variety of different text-types;
- critical reflection on and response to texts;
- discussion which encompasses different interpretations of and responses to text.

What Do We Know About Writing?

Children's writing develops when they are engaged in authentic written language tasks for a variety of purposes that are clear to them. Teachers have the dual responsibility of planning situations and activities to facilitate this development while being flexible enough to capitalise on opportunities as they arise incidentally during the day to capture the 'teachable moments'. A well-balanced program would include opportunities for children to take an active responsibility for their language learning in a supportive environment where the teacher responds to children's needs and demonstrates how language is used. Children will need time to engage in personal reading and writing on topics of their choice as well as reading and writing across the curriculum.

The Writing Developmental Continuum provides strategies directly related to children's phases of development. Teachers should, however, plan time for modelled, shared, guided and individual writing and reading, and time to talk about what is to be done and how to do it. The emphasis or teaching focus will change according to the students' needs, but all of these essential elements will help children make the links between oral and written texts, and see the relationship among form, purpose and audience. These understandings are critical to the development of writing.

One aim of teaching is to help children become independent learners. This can only happen if teachers allow children to make decisions and take responsibility for their learning. As part of this process, children can be involved in self-evaluation if teachers promote a positive learning environment where individual achievement is valued more than competition and comparisons. By involving students in daily decisions about evaluation and encouraging them to set and review personal goals, teachers can help children to know what they know. Self-evaluation encourages children to think about what they are doing and what they need to do.

Another important, but often neglected, aspect of the language program is sharing time. Sharing time provides opportunities for children to present finished work to an audience or to gauge audience reaction and receive constructive feedback to early drafts of writing. Sharing sessions may be organised for the whole class or small groups. These sessions are highly motivating as children have a real purpose and audience for their productions. Children also learn the appropriate oral language social skills involved in giving and receiving feedback. They become more tolerant and develop respect for the efforts of others. Teachers may need to provide guidance on appropriate behaviour at first and to demonstrate how to ask or answer questions effectively. The sessions also provide opportunities for teachers to observe levels of understanding displayed by individual children and to plan follow-up activities where necessary to consolidate learning. Sharing time encourages children to reflect upon, and share, each other's language work in a community of readers and writers.

Teachers are conscious of the need to generate enthusiasm and interest in language. By approaching language sessions with obvious enjoyment and positive expectations, teachers will help children develop positive attitudes to language learning.

REMEMBER: Teachers do make a difference.

Principles of Writing

This document is based on beliefs that all children need:

- opportunities to write everyday
- to learn to write by writing
- to learn to write by talking about their writing
  (They need to be given opportunities to test their theories about the system of writing.
  Interaction with others will help children make sense of writing and its place in the language.)
- to be aware of adults writing in a variety of contexts for many purposes
- to see regular demonstrations of the writing process
- to be surrounded by a print-rich environment that they helped to create
- to have their writing efforts valued
- to have time to refine their writing, through editing and revising, when writing for publication
- to have time to share their finished writing
- to be encouraged to set personal goals and take responsibility for their writing development
- to reflect on the process of writing
- to write for purposes which are clear to them
- to write for real audiences.

Jacqueline: 'Me and my sister are picking apples.'

Differences Between Oral and Written Language

One of the major tasks confronting children as they learn to write is learning about the differences between the structures of oral and written language. Written language is not just 'talk' written down. Although both speech and writing draw on the same grammatical system, they do so in different ways. That is, we make different grammatical choices according to whether we are talking or writing. Essentially, coming to terms with these differences is the main task children need to learn to write successfully. These differences generally relate to the function or purposes of writing. When writing, it is necessary to provide additional information for the reader, because the reader may not share the context with the writer.

It is important that teachers understand the differences between spoken and written language because this knowledge will enable them to provide children with appropriate assistance when it is needed. When the functions of speech and writing overlap, language structures are likely to be similar. For example, a prepared speech or monologue is likely to have similar structures to spoken language.

In general terms the functions of spoken and written language differ in the following ways:

Spoken texts are used for:

- maintaining personal relationships
- sorting out ideas
- speculating and hypothesising

Written texts are used for:

- recording
- detailing facts
- logical thinking
- reasoning
- reflecting.

The permanence of writing allows written texts to be reflected upon.

Spoken Texts

- are more implicit because they rely on a context that is shared between speaker and listener. This context does not have to be referred to, e.g. 'Get the book from over there!' (pointing)
- often accompany action so that some of the meaning is conveyed by the action, e.g. 'Now move this here. Now over there!'
- have no sentence or word boundaries
- rely on stress, intonation, gesture, facial expression and body language to provide much of the meaning
- are linked from utterance to utterance with respect to the people involved. Intonation and stress are used to change meaning, e.g. 'How are you?', 'I'm okay, where have you been?'
- have fewer content words but contain a lot of structural words (conjunctions, pronouns, articles, prepositions)

Written Texts

- are more explicit because references to the context need to be included in the text, e.g. The teacher told the child to get the book from the table
- are always removed from the situation to which they refer and so must include contextual details, e.g. He told him to put the chess piece on the right-hand square
- organise language into words, sentences and paragraphs. These are not natural but are imposed by the written language system being used.
- rely on punctuation, word order and word choice (adjectives, adverbs, similes and metaphors) to provide meaning, e.g. 'Shut the door!' she snapped angrily, with the voice of a sergeant major.
- are composed in sentences and are usually organised with respect to the topic. Punctuation and text structure are used to help order ideas. Sentence themes can be reorganised to change meaning, e.g. Her attention was caught by his strange accent. His strange accent caught her attention.
- have more content words (nouns, verbs, adjectives and adverbs).Written texts are often made denser by turning verbs into nouns (nominalisation), e.g. 'The destruction of the environment was of great concern', is more concise than, 'People were very concerned about the way the environment was being destroyed'.

How to Use the Writing Developmental Continuum

Predict where the children are on the Continuum by looking at the Key Indicators

Collect Data to confirm the prediction, through observation and collection of work samples

Involve parents and children

Link Assessment with Teaching by referring to the major teaching emphases

Monitor and Plan by ongoing collection of data, consultation with parents and linking children's current phase of development with teaching.

Predict

- Read through the Overview of the Writing Developmental Continuum, with special reference to the Phase Descriptions and Key Indicators.
- Match your knowledge of the children in your class with the Phase Descriptions and Key Indicators to predict which phase each child is operating in. Experience shows that it takes about thirty seconds to place a child on the Continuum in this way.

Collect Data

The Continuum indicators will help you gather information about children's writing behaviours. Your data collection will be carried out as you observe children writing and collect samples of their writing during regular classroom activities, writing for a range of purposes and audiences.

Place Children on the Continuum

- Children who are beginning to demonstrate any writing-like behaviours are operating in the Role Play Writing Phase, although they may not yet exhibit all the Key Indicators. Beyond the Role Play phase children are said to be working in a phase when they exhibit all the Key Indicators of that phase. In the last resort the placement of the child in a phase will rest upon the teacher's professional judgement.

- For most of the children in a class it is only necessary to look at the Key Indicators.
- If teachers choose to look at more than the Key Indicators, they will expect and find that children may display behaviours across two or three phases. It is the Key Indicators, however, that determine which phase they are in. This information is designed to inform and guide your teaching program.
- For children who are at risk and are experiencing difficulties teachers may wish to look at all the indicators because:
  - the indicators comprise a sensitive and fine-grained diagnostic tool that enables teachers to focus on children's current understandings and the strategies they are using. The information obtained provides an individualised guide to teaching
  - it is sometimes difficult to measure the progress of children at risk and it may appear that they are making little or no progress. If all the indicators are used it is encouraging for teachers, parents and the children themselves to be aware of the tiny but crucial gains that are actually being made
  - it is sometimes tempting to talk about a child at risk in terms of what he or she cannot do. A focus on the achievement of behavioural indicators leads to a celebration of what that child can do and how much she or he is learning.
- If a class contains several children at risk, it is suggested that the teacher observes only one of these children for at least two weeks before moving on to the next child.

Involve Parents and Children

Parents will often have a very clear and accurate sense of their children's competencies. They are usually pleased to be asked to comment on what they have observed at home. Including parents in the assessment and monitoring process by asking for their observations may help you to gain an extremely accurate picture of the children.

Children are also keenly interested in their own progress and enjoy using the list of indicators for children entitled *Things I Can Do* (see pages 112–119).

Once parents are able to see where their children are placed on the Continuum they will be interested in reading the page of ideas which suggest how they might like to support their children's development at home.

Link Assessment with Teaching

When children are placed in phases, the section entitled Major Teaching Emphases will guide the selection of appropriate teaching strategies and activities. Many of these are described in some detail in this book. Others are discussed in the accompanying First Steps *Writing: Resource Book*. The key teaching strategies described in each phase are considered to be critical for children's further development. They can be used to meet the needs of a whole class, small groups and individual children.

Monitor Progress

The Developmental Continuum provides a sensitive and accurate means by which progress can be monitored over time. This involves further observation and data collection. Links will constantly be made between assessment and teaching.

The writing record forms at the back of the book may be used to map individual or class progress.

Part III

Phases of Writing Development

By scanning the phase descriptions and key indicators in the overview sheet at the beginning of this book, teachers can place children in a phase of the Writing Continuum. Placement can be validated by examining samples of children's work. Part III of this book provides details of each phase, including all indicators and a wide range of appropriate teaching strategies.

Teachers will find the Writing Developmental Continuum will help them to monitor children's writing development. It should be noted, however, that all the subtleties of fine writing can not be captured by any one set of indicators. Teachers are therefore cautioned to ensure that creativity and individuality are fostered at all times, in conjunction with those features of writing outlined in this document.

Each phase includes:

- samples of writing that are typical of the phase
- indicators describing children's writing behaviours
  key indicators are marked ◆ *and written in bold print*
- a description of major teaching emphases
- a range of strategies and activities organised under the same headings as indicators in the phase
- children's self-assessment
- notes for parents.

I dreamt that a monster came and stole our radio.

Role Play Writing

Children are beginning to come to terms with a new aspect of language, that of written symbols. They experiment with marks on paper with the intention of communicating a message or emulating adult writing.

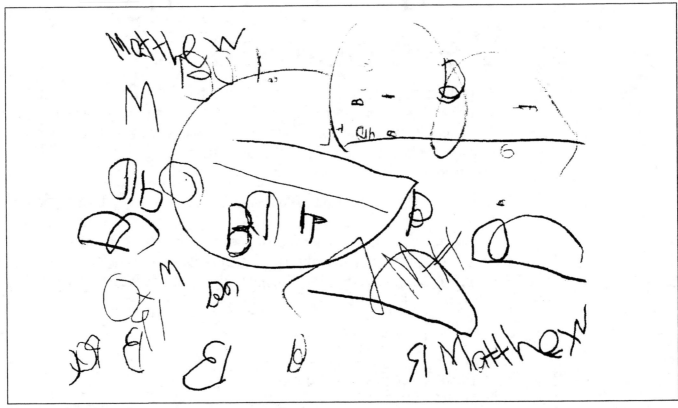

Matthew: 'This says all about the cricket.'

From this sample we can assume that Matthew:

◆ **assigns a message to own symbols**
◆ **is aware that print carries a message**
◆ **understands that writing and drawing are different**
◆ **uses known letters or approximations of letters to represent written language**
• places letters randomly on page
• mixes letters, numerals and invented letter shapes
• flips or reverses letters
• experiments with upper and lower case letters. May show a preference for upper case.
• repeats a few known alphabet symbols, frequently using letters from own name
◆ **shows beginning awareness of directionality**
• attempts to write own name

Role Play Writing Indicators

(See also Phase 1: Preliminary of *Spelling: Developmental Continuum*)

Content, Organisation and Contextual Understandings

(See p. 28)

The writer:

- ◆ **assigns a message to own symbols**
- ◆ **understands that writing and drawing are different, e.g. points to words while 'reading'**
- ◆ **is aware that print carries a message**
- orally recounts own experiences
- knows some favourite parts of stories, rhymes, jingles or songs
- reads text from memory or invents meaning (the meaning may change each time)
- writes and asks others to assign meaning to what has been written
- talks about own drawing and writing
- tells adults what to write, e.g.' This is my cat'
- role plays writing messages for purpose, e.g. telephone messages
- states purpose for own 'writing', e.g. 'This is my shopping list'
- recognises own name (or part of it) in print, e.g. 'My name starts with that'
- attempts to write own name
- thinks own 'writing' can be read by others.

Concepts and Conventions

(See p. 32)

The writer:

- ◆ **uses known letters or approximations of letters to represent written language**
- ◆ **shows beginning awareness of directionality, i.e. points to where print begins**
- draws symbols consisting of straight, curved or intersecting lines that simulate letters
- makes random marks on paper
- produces aimless or circular scribble
- makes horizontal or linear scribble with some breaks
- places letters randomly on page
- writes random strings of letters
- mixes letters, numerals and invented letter shapes
- flips or reverses letters
- makes organisational decisions about writing, e.g. 'I'll start here so it will fit'
- copies layout of some text forms, e.g. letters, lists.

Strategies

(See p. 34)

The writer:

- experiments with upper and lower case letters. May show a preference for upper case
- repeats a few known alphabet symbols frequently using letters from own name
- copies print from environment.

Attitude

(See p. 34)

The writer:

- enjoys stories and asks for them to be retold or re-read
- listens attentively to the telling or reading of stories and other texts
- 'writes' spontaneously for self rather than for an audience.

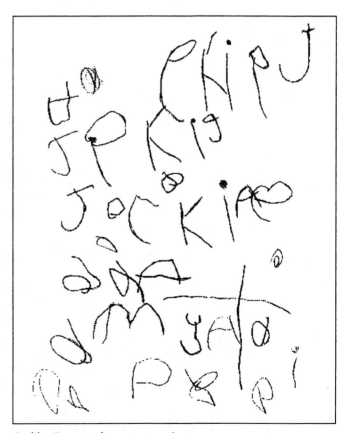

Jackie: 'I can write my name.'

Spelling Indicators

The Key Indicators from the First Steps *Spelling: Developmental Continuum* have been included because learning to spell is part of learning to communicate in written language. For further information about children's spelling development, see the First Steps *Spelling: Developmental Continuum*.

Preliminary Spelling Phase

In this phase children become aware that print carries a message. They experiment with writing-like symbols as they try to represent written language. Their writing is not readable by others as understandings of sound-symbol relationships have yet to develop.

Key Indicators

The writer:

◆ **is aware that print carries a message**
◆ **uses writing-like symbols to represent written language**
◆ **uses known letters or approximations of letters to represent written language**
◆ **assigns a message to own symbols.**

Aaron: 'I made a Superman birthday card for Rhianon.'

Strategies Used by Children

In this phase, children may assign a message to their symbols, e.g. 'This says "Kate"'. However, they do not relate their symbols to particular sounds.

Children use many strategies to help them as they endeavour to come to terms with written language. They copy adults' writing and environmental print. They repeat a few known symbols and talk about what they are doing.

Environmental Print

Children surrounded by print are likely to copy letters in a random way. The letters may be reversed or upside down, and appear in all sorts of places. Children may make no particular meaning from the written symbols or they may assign their own message to the print.

Repetition

Children may focus on certain letter groupings, especially those from their own names, and repeat these to generate a greater quantity of writing.

Talk

Children talk with peers and adults to clarify thinking and meaning. Requests may be made for specific letters or words. The answers to requests may be used by children or discarded as unsuitable to their needs.

Related Activities

Children may draw and tell about the drawing before attempting any writing. This enables them to clarify their thinking.

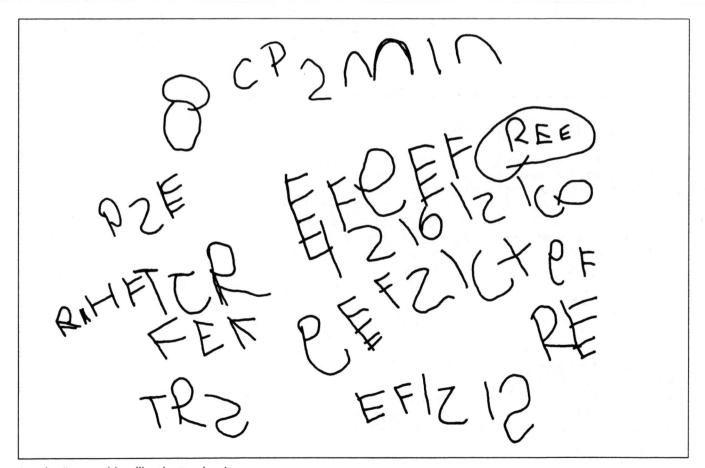

Jasmin: 'I am writing like the teacher.'

Teaching Notes

Language skills develop when children are active participants in their own learning. Children need opportunities to interact with peers and adults so that they can question, confirm and add to their language knowledge base. Questions about language should be answered at the time of request.

In this phase, children need to understand the precise connection between oral and written language; i.e. speech can be written down and read back. Children also need help to develop the concept of a letter and a word. A flexible teaching program will allow children every opportunity to develop these understandings.

Consistent aspects of language are taught first, e.g. the letter name, not the sound it represents in a particular word.

Children gain understanding when writing is modelled daily in a meaningful context and the purpose for writing is clearly stated. Modelled writing can be used to demonstrate the interrelationship of reading, writing, speaking and listening.

Children respond to environmental print that is meaningful to them, e.g. songs or rhymes learned could be displayed and referred to regularly by children and teachers.

Children need many opportunities to write.

Major Teaching Emphases

- ◆ **demonstrate the connection between oral and written language**
- ◆ **demonstrate that written messages remain constant**
- ◆ **demonstrate that writing communicates a message**
- ◆ **focus on the way print works (print concepts and conventions)**
- ◆ **demonstrate that writing is purposeful and has an intended audience**
- ◆ **use correct terminology for letters, sounds, words**
- ◆ **encourage children to experiment with writing**
- • focus on language structures and features through songs, stories and poems
- • encourage children to talk about environmental print
- • focus on alphabet knowledge (letter names)
- • help children develop a stable concept of a word

At all phases:
- ◆ **model good English language use**
- ◆ **model writing every day**
- ◆ **encourage students to reflect on their understandings, gradually building a complete picture of written language structures**
- ◆ **ensure that students have opportunities to write for a variety of audiences and purposes**
- ◆ **encourage students to share their writing experiences.**

◆ *Entries in bold are considered critical to the children's further development*

Establishing an Environment for Language Learning

Children respond positively to teachers who aim to create a love of writing and reading by providing an interesting and enjoyable language program and showing the pleasure they derive from reading and writing. The classroom environment should provide relevant examples of language, how it looks, how it works and how it is used. Children need to experiment with writing through meaningful activities and their efforts should be accepted and praised. They learn to write by experimenting with writing, talking about writing and watching others write. Interaction and positive responses are critical during this phase. A non-threatening atmosphere is comfortable for all participants.

Ways to Create an Environment for Language Learning

- Provide time for daily, shared and independent reading and writing. Immerse children in oral and written language.
- Respond to the oral or 'written' message rather than the structure or form.
- Take every opportunity to provide and promote books and magazines of interest to children.
- Encourage parent helpers to participate in discussion and conversations with children.
- Establish a writing centre with a variety of paper, pencils and crayons. Have a board nearby so that children are able to display their writing if they choose to do so.
- Write children's names on cards. Place the cards around the room.
- Provide contexts and purposes for introducing different forms of writing, e.g. a science table with labelled exhibits, a special days calendar, note pads for shopping lists in the class shop, telephone message pads and so on.
- Display the names of the days of the week.
- Teach children to change the weather chart. Discuss the weather as you write the weather report for the day. Read with the class. Keep a weather book for a season by gluing the daily reports into a scrapbook. Provide opportunities for children to use a computer to print out weather reports independently.
- Make a birthday pictograph and/or chart to show when each child's birthday occurs. Share birthday invitations and cards.
- Make alphabet and number cards available to the children.

- Have a shelf to display local newspaper articles as they are a source of interesting news for children. Papers often contain photographs or articles about people known to them. Ask the local distributor for copies to be delivered.
- Make available old telephone books, street directories and other reference material for purposeful play activities.
- Write notes, memos and reminders. Encourage children to try to read the notes and recall their contents and purpose.

Content, Organisation and Contextual Understandings

(See p. 23)

Children need to understand what writing is, and why we write. They need to see others reading and writing. They need opportunities to talk about direct experiences, retell simple stories, discuss new vocabulary and engage in role-play activities. This interaction will help children clarify their understandings and order their ideas.

Modelled and Shared Writing

Modelled writing is a means of demonstrating the processes and products of writing. The teacher 'thinks aloud' while writing for the audience of children and shows how writers make selections about what to write and how to write.

Shared writing differs from modelled writing in that the teacher retains ownership of the writing, but works collaboratively with children asking for ideas and accepting some of their suggestions. The final decision about what to write remains with the teacher but the process allows for discussion and explanation related to writing.

- Write about shared experiences and display writing for children to read later, e.g. 'A big truck came to deliver sand today'. Re-read the writing many times.
- Compile a class news book scribing children's own news. Invite the newstellers to draw a picture for their news and write their name on the page.
- Write known or new nursery rhymes as children watch and encourage children to join in 'reading'. Collect the rhymes and make into a book of 'Our Rhymes'.
- Demonstrate writing of different forms, e.g. labels for the science table exhibit, recipes for cooking, thank-you letters to helpers, lists for shopping, messages to parents.
- Sometimes write messages on the board, repeating each word as it is written.
- Sometimes write children's sentences as they dictate.
- Brainstorm class instructions and write them as children watch, e.g. 'Feed the guinea pigs every day'.

Teaching Emphases

Use modelled and shared writing to help children develop understanding that:

- writing can be used for different purposes and audiences
- there is a connection between written and oral language
- writers make selections about how and what to write
- writing can be modified
- own experiences are a source of writing
- writing can be read by others.

Independent Writing

Children begin to 'write' long before they have control over the mechanics of writing. They need to build on what they already know and to puzzle out the written language system. The classroom can provide many opportunities and reasons to write and children should be allowed to make real choices and to act on these choices. The more children write the more they focus on print and the ways in which print can be used to fulfil their needs.

Use independent writing opportunites to expose children to a range of contexts so that children have many opportunities to use writing for their own purposes and audiences.

Suggested teaching strategies to promote independent writing:

- Respond to the message children have written.
- Encourage children to write for themselves each day.
- Celebrate children's individual writing efforts and display writing.
- Share real writing with children, e.g. letters you receive.

- Provide particular situations that enable children to write for a purpose and suggest different types of writing that could be tried, e.g. a letter to someone, a message, a birthday card. Encourage children to write their own name on drawings and pictures.
- Talk with children about their 'writing' and encourage them to 'read' it.
- Encourage children to write and draw after hearing a story.
- Encourage children to problem solve by working out how to write something, then praise their efforts.

Some contexts for independent writing:

'The Writing Bag'
Equip a small 'back pack' or school bag with interesting articles that could be used for writing:
- a range of plain, lined and coloured paper
- recycled greeting cards
- envelopes
- pencils and felt pens
- pencil sharpener and eraser
- an alphabet chart
- a brief note to parents to explain the function of the bag.

Encourage children to take turns to take the bag home for one night and return the next day to show and tell about the writing they have done at home.

'Personal Notebooks'
Make small notebooks available for each child and encourage children to write in them.

'The Writing Centre'
- typewriters and word processors
- picture dictionaries
- a range of writing equipment
- a display board
- a writing desk with chairs
- alphabet cards and charts
- a few books and magazines of interest to children

'The Reading Corner'
- picture dictionaries
- paper and pencils
- library cards
- card for bookmarks
- notebooks or charts for children to record their names

'The Class Shop'
- note pad, pencils, signs 'shop open' or 'shop closed'
- telephone and message book
- magnetic letters, board prices and sale tickets
- household articles that display labels, brands etc.
- 'for sale' articles written by the children
- magazines and newspaper clippings
- posters
- play money

'The Doctor's Surgery'
- an appointment book
- telephone and pad
- 'Doctor In' — 'Doctor out' sign
- an alphabet or picture eye chart
- poster showing the human body and labelled parts

'The Fire Station'
- signs, e.g. 'Fire Station', 'This way out', 'Alarm'
- labelled maps of the classroom for use in locating fires
- a log book of 'fires'

'The Home Corner'
- shopping lists, telephone book, children's names and addresses, recipe books, message board

'The Post Office'
- note paper
- envelopes and stamps
- post box
- post bag, letters for sorting.

Teaching Emphases

Encourage children to:
- initiate own writing activities
- learn to write by writing
- emulate what they see peers and adults write
- apply, practise and refine understandings gained through shared and modelled reading and writing
- experiment with print to work out concept and conventions of written language
- begin to match oral to written language and explore how words are represented in print
- write their own name
- use environmental print as models for own writing.

Modelled and Shared Reading

Reading to children is a way of extending shared reading experiences they have had at home. Reading a range of different texts will help children understand that books are written for different purposes and audiences and are constructed differently.

- Read Stories to children just for fun.
- Choose books that have natural language.
- Read the same book several times and make it available for children to read independently.
- Actively promote books by sharing your own enjoyment of them.

- Involve children in talk about books in which the illustrations support the text.
- Use large print books and point to words as you read them.
- Ask children to make predictions before you read. Encourage children to look at the cover, the author, the title, the blurb for clues.
- Read books which have clear information and logical sequences.
- Share both narrative and informational texts. Read favourite poems and ryhmes.
- Read books that children bring.
- Read functional print such as notices, recipes, instructions in the context of the program.
- Share timetable and rosters with children. Refer to calender and mark important events.
- Read books that feature rhyme, rhythm and repetition and predictable text so that children can join in freely.
- Use large print books to draw attention to various aspects of print. Point and 'think aloud' while reading. Encourage children to predict outcomes and compare their predictions with the text. Discuss children's predictions, giving positive feedback and praise for children's efforts.
- Share greeting cards, messages and letters with children.
- Praise children when they:
  - identify letters that occur in their own name
  - identify other words which start with the same letter as their name
  - point to and name letters in words from shared books or other sources
  - identify words
  - match words from different sources
- Read familiar rhymes and leave the last word for children to say.
- Compare the layout and structure of fiction and non-fiction books, and discuss the features of each. Comment about the layout of the text and pictures.
- Tell or read a story and discuss the sequence of events. Use picture cues. Have children retell the story. Give some structure to the retell by encouraging children to consider who was in the story, when and where it happened and the events in sequence. Ask children how they felt about the story.
  Discuss how the pictures relate to the text.
- Encourage talk about text innovation from known texts, e.g. re-reading the story, changing the characters or the outcome.
- When reading, sometimes choose stories that lend themselves to story maps, e.g. *Little Red Riding Hood*. Work with children to chart a story map. Use a related concept keyboard overlay to reinforce the sequence. Ensure there is a logical sequence. In some stories, e.g.

Chicken Licken, the sequence does not affect the outcome, whereas in *The Three Little Pigs*, it does.
- Talk about a sequence of events when conducting language experience activities, e.g. 'First we put the flour in the bowl. After that we added the milk'. Involve children in recalling information orally.
- Assist children to arrange simple pictures in a sequence and have cards or other games which involve children in considering the order of events.
- Teach children to chant and sing repetitive rhymes and songs, and display for future use.
- Discuss children's news and ask for additional information such as when or where the events occurred, to raise children's awareness of audience needs.
- Involve children in picture talks.
- Encourage children to discuss their paintings, etc. Often, children will talk as they draw. Add written text to children's work when appropriate.
- Include simple computer software that children can use individually or with a group

Teaching Emphases

Use shared and modelled reading to develop children's understanding that:

- people read for different purposes
- information texts are different from narrative texts
- authors choose different layouts for books
- many stories follow a recognisable pattern of orientation, complication and resolution
- pictures complement written texts
- own experiences are a source of writing
- some texts represent people similar to those they know, and other texts do not.

Independent Reading

Use independent reading opportunities to allow children to clarify understandings of the way in which print works.
- Have an attractive book corner that is easily accessible to children and frequently introduce new material.
- Provide a range of written material in different genres.
- Provide alphabet friezes.
- Display children's names.
- Create an environment that is rich in functional print, e.g. labels, signs, charts of known songs and poems, helper's rosters, instructions for use of equipment.
- Provide access to taped stories with accompanying texts.
- Equip focus with a range of relevant texts, e.g.

  'The cooking area'
  - commercial and class recipe books
  - safety charts
  - a list of clean up duties
  - food charts
  - lists of equipment

  'The doctor's surgery'
  - magazines
  - eye test charts
  - health posters
  - instructions from medicines

Strategies
- Draw attention to and use labels and signs in the classroom and outside.
- Encourage children to read signs when on excursions.
- Print songs and poems on to individual cards and place in an attractive labelled box. Encourage children to 'read' them.
- Use an easel with large sheets of paper and write messages each day. Leave each message and add a new one. Repeat the sentence pattern and varying one or two words each day. Include key pictures. For example:
  - Please help tidy the blocks today.
  - Please help tidy the Post Office today.
  - Please help tidy the cooking area today.

Teaching Emphases

Encourage children to:
- initiate own reading activities
- relate reading to writing
- apply, practise and refine understandings gained through shared and modelled reading and writing.

Concepts and Conventions

(See p. 23)

Shared reading can be used to introduce many concepts and conventions of print. It should be remembered, however, that the main purpose of sharing literature is enjoyment, and teaching points should not dominate or intrude upon this. In this phase, children need a variety of opportunities to develop concepts of print through play and informal talk. Use incidental opportunities to develop children's interest in words and letters.

Children need to understand how print is organised to make progress in their own writing. Modelled writing, shared writing and shared reading provide ideal opportunities for teachers to develop children's awareness of various concepts and conventions of print. Personal or independent writing allows children to experiment with print, and puzzle out solutions to writing and spelling problems as they occur. Children's queries about the language system provide opportunities for discussion with a view to helping them problem solve to find a solution. Children's talk about language should be valued and fostered.

- Make incidental references to words, spaces, letters, lines of print, left to right, top to bottom direction of print.
- Count the words in a line of print or clap for each word spoken to help develop the children's concept of a word.
- Use a variety of incidental activities to develop the concept of a letter, e.g. play with letter cards, magnetic letters, plasticine letters and alphabet games. Refer to magazines, papers and concept keyboard programs.
- Discuss the feature of books: mention such features as the cover, title, author, illustrator, contents page, pictures and diagrams.
- Draw attention to special print used in books, e.g. 'down' may be printed down the page. This often provides a discussion point for the children and they may copy the idea into their 'writing'.
- Point out, and talk about, print in the environment.
- Use name cards, nursery rhymes etc. to help children recognise words that are important to them.
- Talk about children's own writing and drawings to help them differentiate between the two.
- Use environmental print to make incidental references to words, spaces, letters, lines of print.
- Model the use of conventions such as full stops, commas, capital letters in context.
- Write a child's news sentence on to sentence strips. Cut one sentence into individual words and encourage children to match words to the sentence strip.

Children in this phase have not made the connection between the written symbol and the sound that it represents. Teachers need to help them make the connection.

The following activities are suggested to help children connect symbols to the sounds they represent. It is not intended that letters and sounds be taught in isolation.

- Display, and incidentally refer to, alphabet letter names.
- Incidentally refer to letter-sound relationships.
- Introduce alphabet songs and jingles.
- Introduce nursery rhymes. Chart and display for children's reference.
- Discuss and comment on the children's use of letters or approximation, e.g. 'That looks like an E. E is the first letter of your name, Ellen'.
- Play games that involve sounds, rhymes and rhythms.
- Play oral cloze games in which children predict rhyming patterns in familiar texts.
- Use puzzles and riddles in which children are involved in problem solving to discover specific sounds or letters.
- Have special letter days; i.e. ask children to bring along anything which starts with a particular letter. Label and display articles.
- Provide time each day for children to play with, and manipulate, language.
- Provide activities that give children the opportunity to distinguish between letters and numerals.
- Play 'I Spy'.
- Use children's names to start discussions, e.g. 'Who else has a name that starts with the letter...?'

The First Steps *Spelling: Developmental Continuum* provides more detailed information about the teaching of sound-symbol relationships.

Teaching Emphases

These suggestions are to help children develop understanding that:

- the message is in the print.
- messages can be written.
- print carries a constant message.
- print goes left to right, top to bottom.
- a word is a unit of print with space on either side.
- a word consists of letters.
- terms such as word, letter, capital letter, sentence are used about print.
- punctuation is used in written text.
- initial letters are those that you see first.
- a letter can represent a range of sounds.
- words may rhyme.

Strategies and Attitudes

(See p. 23)

- Share feelings about writing, e.g. excitement, pleasure, apprehension, sense of pride and success.
- Encourage children to share their 'writing' and to tell others what they have discovered.
- Share real writing such as letters, greeting cards and notes.
- Model processes of reflective thinking, for instance after modelling writing 'I think that sounds right now. I had to go over it a couple of times to get it right.'
- Help children to use environmental print by modelling how this can be done, i.e. locating letters or words to use in writing.
- Emphasise the value and importance of taking risks and having-a-go at writing.

Teaching Emphases

In this phase children need to be encouraged to:

- have-a-go at writing
- use own experiences as a source of ideas for writing
- use environmental print
- use talk to help make decisions about what to write
- believe that writing is fun.

For Parents

How can I help my child with writing?

- Find time to show children that you value reading and writing for yourself, and share reading and writing with them. Reading teaches children many things about writing and experimenting with writing helps children develop their understandings about reading.
- Take children to the library and encourage them to select their own books.
- Share simple picture storybooks whenever you can. Talk about the pictures and story and relate events or characters to your child's experiences. Encourage questions and predictions about the stories.
- Read and sing nursery rhymes with children. Use as many action rhymes as possible, such as 'one little piggy went to market' or 'pattacake…'
- Read books which feature rhyme and repitition. Sometimes point to the words as they are read. Encourage children to join in and to predict which words come next.
- Talk about the events of the day encouraging children to join in.
- Talk about print in the environment, e.g. stop signs, advertisments.
- Show children how you use writing. Write messages, shopping lists, telephone messages, letters and greeting cards in front of the children and talk about what you are doing.
- Provide a special place for children to write. Equipment such as a small table or desk, an easel-type blackboard and a notice board for displaying writing plus a range of writing materials such as scrap paper (lined, coloured or plain), used greeting cards, crayons, bank forms, mail order forms, envelopes and little note-books would provide an excellent environment for children to experiment with writing.
- Find opportunities to display children's names.
- When children ask about letters of the alphabet, call the letters by their names not the sounds they may represent.
- Talk about alphabet books and answer children's questions.
- Provide magnetic or plastic letter tiles for children's play.
- Allow children to use a typewriter or word processor to play with and write messages. They may discover some letters from their name.
- Write messages for children to read, e.g. Please feed the cat, Kim. Please phone Nanna.
- Play rhyming games like 'I spy…'

- Respond positively to the message in your children's 'writing' rather than the letter formations or spelling. Celebrate children's efforts and encourage them to have-a-go at writing.

Becky: 'I made my shopping list.'

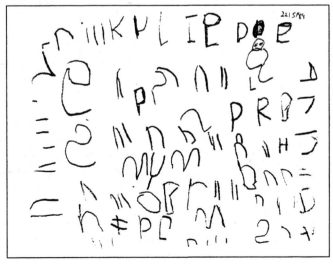

Kylie: 'I am writing my mum a letter.'

Becky and Kylie know a lot about written language. They need encouragement to continue their development.

Experimental Writing

Children are aware that speech can be written down and that written messages remain constant. They understand the left to right organisation of print and experiment with writing letters and words.

SHARON'S LETTER

To tooth fairy can you give me 2 dollars because I only got 50 cents and I pulled it out but I couldn't eat or drink I pulled it out in the middle of me cleaning my teeth

Love from Sharon. Do you like me. Write here ——— but if you don't like me you can't take it

X O X O

> tog tooth ferecan uoy give me 2 boles bekos I onLe got 2osents and I Pellb it oot but I cooent et ow bring I PPeleb it owt in the mibeⒶll othme Klening MI teth Love fron Sharon, dⓞoo uoy Lick me ritⓣa hiar ——— xoxo xoxo xoto but if uoy bont Lick me takit uⓘⓨ krn

Sharon, age 7, exhibits all Key Indicators from the Experimental Phase and some from the Early Writing Phase. This is to be expected as children learn more about written language. Sharon:

- ◆ **reads back own writing**
- ◆ **attempts familiar forms of writing, e.g. letters**
- ◆ **uses writing to convey meaning**
- • writes to communicate messages, direct experiences or feelings
- ◆ **writes using simplified oral language structures, e.g. 'I brt loles'**

- ◆ **realises that print contains a constant message**
- • tells others what has been written
- ◆ **uses left to right and top to bottom orientation of print**
- • distinguishes between numerals and letters
- ◆ **demonstrates one-to-one correspondence between written and spoken word**
- • leaves a space between word-like clusters of letters
- • writes spontaneously for self or chosen audience.

Experimental Writing Indicators

(See also Phase 2: Semi-Phonetic Spelling and Phase 3: Phonetic Spelling of *Spelling: Developmental Continuum*)

Content, Organisation and Contextual Understandings

(See p. 43)

The writer:

◆ **reads back own writing**
◆ **attempts familiar forms of writing, e.g. lists, letters, recounts, stories, messages**
◆ **writes using simplified oral language structures, e.g. 'I brt loles'**
◆ **uses writing to convey meaning**
• voices thoughts while writing
• writes to communicate messages, direct experiences or feelings
• assumes that reader shares the context so may not give sufficient background information, e.g. may tell 'who' but not 'when'
• often begins sentence with 'I' or 'We'
• is beginning to use written language structures. Has a sense of sentence, i.e. writes complete sentences with or without punctuation
• repeats familiar words when writing, e.g. cat, cat, cat
• generates writing by repeating the same beginning patterns, e.g. 'I like cats, I like dogs, I like birds ...'
• recognises some words and letters in context
• recognises that people use writing to convey meaning.

Concepts and Conventions

(See p. 47)

The writer:

◆ **realises that print contains a constant message**
◆ **uses left to right and top to bottom orientation of print**
◆ **demonstrates one-to-one correspondence between written and spoken words**
• uses upper and lower case letters indiscriminately
• distinguishes between numerals and letters
• leaves a space between word-like clusters of letters
• dictates slowly so teacher can 'keep up' while scribing.

Strategies

(See p. 50)

The writer:

◆ **relies heavily on the most obvious sounds of a word**
• tells others what has been written
• asks others what has been written

• traces and copies letters with some successful formations
• points to 'words' while reading own writing
• voices thoughts while writing
• reads back what has been written to clarify meaning
• experiments with, and overgeneralises print conventions, e.g. puts a full stop after each word
• uses knowledge of rhyme to spell words written
• uses print resources in classroom, e.g. charts, signs, word banks.

Attitude

(See p. 50)

The writer:

• listens attentively to the telling or reading of stories and other texts
• writes spontaneously for self or chosen audience.

Kristy: 'I brought pusses.'

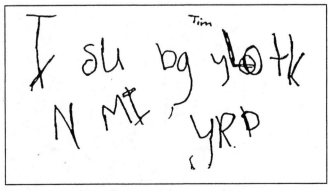

Tim: 'I saw a big yellow truck in my yard.'

Spelling Indicators

The key indicators from the First Steps *Spelling: Developmental Continuum* have been included because learning to spell is part of learning to communicate in written language. For further information about children's spelling development, see the First Steps *Spelling: Developmental Continuum*.
Children in the Experimental Writing Phase may be in the Semi-phonetic or Phonetic Spelling Phase.

Semi-Phonetic Spelling Phase

In this phase, children show developing understanding of sound-symbol relationships. Their spelling attempts show evidence of sound-symbol correspondence. They may represent a word with one, two or three letters.

Key Indicators

The writer:

◆ **uses left to right and top to bottom orientation of print**

◆ **relies on the sounds which are most obvious to him or her. This may be the initial sound, initial and final sounds, or initial, medial and final**

sounds e.g. D (down), DN (down), DON (down), KT (kitten), WT (went), BAB (baby), LRFT (elephant)

◆ **represents a whole word with one, two or three letters. Uses mainly consonants, e.g. kgr (kangaroo), BT (bit)**

Phonetic Spelling Phase

In this phase, children are able to provide an almost perfect match between letters and sounds. Letters are chosen on the basis of sound, often without regard for conventional letter patterns. Spelling attempts are meaningful and becoming more like standard spelling.

Key Indicators

The child:

◆ **chooses letters on the basis of sound without regard for conventional spelling patterns, e.g. kaj (cage), tabl (table), birgla (burglar), vampia (vampire), pepl (people), sum (some), bak (back)**

◆ **sounds-out and represents all substantial sounds in a word, e.g. kitn (kitten), wacht (watched), anathe (another), aftrwoods (afterwards), siclon (cyclone), spidr (spider), isgrem (icecream), necst (next), peepl (people)**

◆ **develops particular spellings for certain sounds often using self-formulated rules, e.g. becoz (because)/woz (was), wher (were)/whas (was), dor (door)/sor (saw)/mor (more), hape (happy)/fune (funny), poot (put)/wood (would)**

This note was found in the doctor's surgery corner at preschool.

Doctor went out
Come back at one o'clock
1 tablet
1 Pill

Strategies Used by Children

In this phase, children are aware that printed messages remain constant and are developing an awareness of the relationship of symbols to the sounds they represent.

Children use many strategies to help them as they endeavour to come to terms with written language. They copy environmental print, repeat known symbols, talk about what they are doing and use their current knowledge of the spelling system.

Environmental Print

Children are likely to copy print and translate it to fulfil their own needs. They sometimes copy lists of words to represent a story form. They recognise some common words and use them in their writing.

Drawing

Children often draw to help them decide what to include in their writing.

Talk

Children are willing to share efforts with others and seek feedback from peers and teacher, e.g. 'What does this say?' 'How do you write 'mummy'?' Composing aloud also helps them to structure their writing.

Repetition

Children are interested in generating longer pieces of writing so they may focus on, and repeat, known words or letter patterns. They frequently use letters from their own names. Some children repeat sentence beginnings and change one word. For example:

> This is my house.
> This is my dog.
> This is my cat.
> or
> I like trucks.
> I like football.
> I like bananas.

Invented Spelling

Children may use two or three letters to represent the whole word. They use significant combinations of consonants and vowels. Letter names are often used for the sound or syllable. Typically, children will say the word to themselves, isolate the first phoneme and choose a suitable letter to represent it. They then write the chosen letter, say the word again, and select the next salient letter, continuing until the word has been completed.

Rebel has overgeneralised his knowledge of full stops.

Rebel: *When a monkey came to my house it was going to eat all my bananas. It will. I was angry yesterday.*

Teaching Notes

Experimental writers need time to explore the writing process. They need to talk with the teacher and their peers.

Shared and modelled reading and writing sessions in meaningful contexts will help children see reading and writing as worthwhile and desirable.

Young children need to experiment with written and oral language, enabling them to understand that words can be written down and that written messages remain constant. Children must feel they can take risks with their use of written language and that their approximations will be accepted.

Teachers can foster children's desire to write by focusing on the message rather than the mechanics of writing. Enabling children to talk about their writing and their message helps them clarify their thoughts. Written responses from the teacher provide a model and motivate further writing.

Children need opportunities to share their writing and to share decisions made during writing sessions. They may discuss the difficulties encountered, ideas for future writing sessions, how correct spelling was achieved and so on.

As children begin to focus on specific sound-symbol relationships, the teaching focus should also change. In the previous phase, the main focus was on the linking of oral to written language. While this focus is still very important, and needs to be reiterated, additional attention is now placed on the sounds and structures of written words. Allow children to problem solve in order to work out how to write the required words, e.g. 'That sound is the same as the first letter in your name'.

Teachers can assist children to become independent writers through the careful use of questions during teacher-student conferences.

Major Teaching Emphases

◆ **model brief, imaginative and factual texts and explain the purpose and intended audience**
◆ **help children build lists of high-frequency words from their reading and writing**
◆ **demonstrate the one-to-one correspondence of written and spoken words**
◆ **discuss how writing can be used to communicate over time and distance**
◆ **encourage children to talk about their experiences**
◆ **help children understand how written texts are composed in sentences**
◆ **help children develop a stable concept of a word**
◆ **help children relate written symbols to the sounds they represent**
◆ **talk about letters, words and sentences**
• help children to segment words into their component sounds
• help children with letter formations

At all phases:

◆ **model good English language use**
◆ **model writing every day**
◆ **encourage students to reflect on their understandings, gradually building a complete picture of written language structures**
◆ **ensure that students have opportunities to write for a variety of audiences and purposes**
◆ **encourage students to share their writing experiences.**

◆ *entries in bold are considered critical to the children's further development*

Establishing an Environment for Language Learning

It is important that teachers establish an environment that encourages experimenting and risk-taking as students explore the writing process. Teachers who expect that writing should always be neat and accurate may discourage writers who are trying to make sense of the systems of language. This can lead to children refusing to write independently or only writing words they can spell or becoming safe, unimaginative writers.

Teachers can nurture, encourage and sustain writing in the classroom if they expect that all children will become writers and endeavour to provide opportunities for purposeful writing each day. Children must understand and value why they are writing so they see a need to undertake the process.

Ways to Create an Environment for Language Learning

- Immerse children in oral and written language
- Provide contexts for introducing different forms of writing, e.g. recipes, letters or invitations
- Set up a class library that contains a variety of reading materials both commercially produced and produced by class members.
- Create a print-rich environment. Display books, children's work and functional written material (jointly constructed by children and teacher), e.g. class rules, word charts, labels, rosters, etc.
- Make available an interesting range of writing materials.
- Provide interesting corners or centres to stimulate discussion and activities.
- Set up a post box to encourage children to write to each other.
- Display charts of poems and songs children have learned.
- Make available a range of dictionaries and other word sources.
- Allow children to have some choice in what they will read and write.
- Plan experiences that will enrich children's language knowledge and provide a shared context for spoken and written activities to follow.
- Plan writing experiences across the curriculum. Collect resources to support writing activities.
- Create 'wall stories'. These can be continuous accounts of a class project. Add pages as the project progresses. When completed, the pages can be collated and made into a big book for the class library.
- Provide opportunities for drama and puppetry.

- Involve children in the decisions to be made in the classroom.
- Use oral news sessions to motivate children to write their news (a recount or a description).
- Encourage parental support for the school language program.
- Write messages to children just for fun.
- Give feedback that is meaningful, e.g. I like the way you wrote 'BIG' in large letters.
- Allow time for sharing writing.
- Conduct sharing circles so that children can receive feedback from peers. Ask: 'Are there any questions or suggestions?'

Content, Organisation and Contextual Understandings

(See p. 37)

Many children have the desire to write for themselves and others. This can be fostered by encouraging children to experiment with writing and by concentrating on the message in the writing.

Shared reading followed by discussions about characters, setting and sequence of events will help children develop a sense of story. Expository texts should also be read and followed by discussions about the content and organisation of the text.

The following activities in context, will help children to see how writing is composed and organised.

Modelled and Shared Writing

An easel that supports large sheets of paper, placed at children's eye level is an ideal place to demonstrate the processes and products of writing. The teacher 'thinks aloud' while writing for the audience of children and shows how writers make a selection about what to write and how to write. Children are encouraged to assist the teacher to find solutions to writing problems. The focus should be chosen to suit the needs of the audience. In this phase, children need to see that writing is a natural and functional part of language development and that ideas are ordered in a planned way. They also need to become aware of decisions faced by writers during the composition process. Modelled writing sessions are short and focused.

- Demonstrate thinking, planning, writing and editing processes.
- Model a variety of written forms.
- Use shared experiences to model writing in a meaningful context e.g. cooking, excursions.
- Write sentences on overhead transparencies, large sheets of paper, the blackboard or in a word processing program.
- Model the use of simple revising and editing activities to demonstrate that changes can be made to a text.
- Model the process of writing as one that may require restructuring to make the meaning clearer.
- Sometimes scribe for children.
- Focus on correct ordering of the text so it makes sense.
- Sometimes take the modelled text through to publication for display in the class library.
- Make big books for sharing and general use.
- Write on a large chart and leave it displayed for the children to read and re-read.

- Try simple text innovation activities after shared reading sessions.
- Write messages to individual children or to the class.
- Write language experience sentences on large sheets of paper or key into a computer and have a hard copy printed. Collate to make a class diary for children to read.
- Create 'wall stories'. These can be continuous accounts of a class project. Add pages as the project progresses. When completed, the pages can be collated and made into a big book for the class library.
- Respond to the message in children's writing by writing a reply or question, rather than always rewriting the child's work correctly. For example:
  Child writes: 'I plad in the yrd.'
  Teacher replies in writing: 'What did you play in the yard?'
  The child is then able to see a model that demonstrates conventional writing in a non-threatening way.
- Model how to find words displayed in the room.
- Model how to choose a topic and how to get help when stuck for ideas.
- Work with children to build class wall dictionaries featuring commonly used words.
- Choose a favourite story, rhyme, song or jingle to use as a text innovation activity. With children, substitute words to change the meaning (but not the pattern) of the text. Some suitable texts are *The Great Big Enormous Turnip*, *The House That Jack Built*, *Three Blind Mice*.
- Write conversations with the whole class, individuals or groups, using an overhead projector, blackboard or paper clipped to an easel.

- Write a question and a child writes the answer. For example:

    Teacher writes: 'What is your name?'

    Child writes: 'My name is Jane'.

    Teacher writes: 'What do you like to do?'

    Structure the questions so reluctant writers can still take part with one-word answers. Accept approximations and congratulate children on their attempts.
- Construct big books based on common experiences or on texts that are known and lend themselves to text innovation. Many books are suitable for this, e.g. *The Musicians of Bremen*, *The Gingerbread Man*. Children write one page each, based on the pattern of the book. Collate the pages into a class book and, with the class, write the introduction and the conclusion.
- Compose texts using picture sequences. This strategy is particularly useful as a way of recording procedures in science, cooking etc. The children can label drawings as a way of refining the information.
- Give children many opportunities to put pictures into a sequence and discuss their reasons for selecting the particular sequence chosen to compose a story.
- Stimulate discussion and generate ideas for writing through picture talks.
- Talk about forms that teachers need to complete, e.g. the weekly return sheet, class roll, money collection sheet, canteen orders etc.
- Plan situations where children work cooperatively in a group on joint writing projects before individual writing sessions. Provide large sheets of paper for group work and allow children to write on the same topic in independent writing time.
- Encourage oral retelling of familiar stories to help children focus on the cohesion of the story.
- Provide opportunities for children to dictate their stories. Some children find this activity satisfying. The way in which children dictate their stories will often give teachers an insight into their understanding of the writing process. Children who dictate one word at a time and wait for it to be written are probably demonstrating that they understand the relationship between the written and the spoken word. Children who present their ideas in a continuous flow may be unsure of the connection between the oral and written word. Dictated stories provide one means of modelling writing. The importance of giving children the opportunity to write daily, however, cannot be overstressed. They need opportunities to experiment and to test their theories.
- Conduct oral news sessions. Select one or two children's news items each day. On a large sheet of paper, write the date and a summary of the child's news. Read each word aloud as you write. Re-read and encourage children to join in. Point to each word as it is read. Cover a word and ask children to predict. Name the news. Type into a computer and print a copy for the news owner to take home. Store all items on computer until there are sufficient news items to make a class news book. Print and photocopy so there are several copies and place on the bookshelf. Share news books with children to promote interest. Place large original sheets in a folder and leave on display at child's eye level. Allow time for the news owners to illustrate their news if they wish. With the children, re-read some news items from the class book each day.
- Make story maps. After reading a story with children, draw a map that shows the setting and captures the events that happened in the story.

Teaching Emphases

Use modelled and shared writing to help children develop understanding that:

- written texts are composed in sentences
- writing can be used to communicate over time and distance, e.g. messages, direct experiences or feelings
- a reader's interpretation of a text is enhanced if the writer includes relevant contextual information
- writers make selection about how and what to write
- writing may need to be modified if it is to be read by others
- the purpose and audience dictate the form which writing takes
- own experiences are a source of writing.

Independent Writing

The following ideas promote independent writing.
- Allow time each day for personal writing.
- Encourage children to share their efforts with peers and adults.
- Encourage children to write reminder notes and messages for themselves, their parents or the class. These can be displayed on a notice board.
- Provide opportunities for children to write labels for displays or signs, or advertisements for coming events.
- Introduce have-a-go pads so children can attempt words they wish to write.
- Encourage children to write recounts after excursions or shared experiences.
- Provide a class letterbox and encourage children to write to each other.
- Display print in different contexts.

Teaching Emphases

Encourage children to:

- initiate their own writing activities
- look for words in the room
- experiment with different written forms they have experienced in modelled and shared writing sessions
- have-a-go at spelling words they need.

Independent Reading

Use independent reading opportunities to allow children to clarify understandings of the way in which print works.

- Have an attractive book corner that is easily accessible to children and frequently introduce new material.
- Provide a range of written material in different genres.
- Provide alphabet friezes, lists of frequently used words, charts of word families.
- Create an environment that is rich in functional print, e.g. labels, signs, charts of known songs and poems, helper's rosters, instructions for use of equipment.
- Provide access to taped stories with accompanying texts.
- Encourage children to publish material and leave it for others to read.
- Equip focus areas with a range of relevant texts, e.g.

    The reading corner'
    - a range of commercial and class-made books
    - magazines
    - book promotional charts
    - author information charts
    - new titles list
    - display board for children's comments on books they have read
    - chart of rules for conduct in reading
    - lists of equipment

    'The science table'
    - magazines
    - information charts
    - labels, captions for exhibits
    - suggestions and instructions for use of equipment
    - posters
    - relevant newspaper articles
- Show children how they may choose books and allow time every day for uninterrupted reading.
- Actively promote new reading material as it becomes available.
- Draw attention to and encourage the use of labels and signs in the classroom and outside.
- Encourage children to read signs when on excursions.

- Print songs and poems on to individual cards and place in an attractive labled box. Encourage children to 'read' them.

Teaching Emphases

Children will:

- initiate own reading activities
- relate reading to writing
- apply, practise and refine understandings gained through shared and modelled reading and writing.

Modelled and Shared Reading

Before reading, involve the children in discussion about such things as the title, author and the suggested content of the book.

After reading, ensure that children have access to the books for individual reading. Audio-taped versions may also be used so that children can listen to a favourite story again and again. Rereading is particularly helpful for children for whom English is a second language.

- Read and reread class-made texts as a shared book experience, or revision, and recall activity, so children can use prediction skills to provide missing information.
- Expose children to a range of literature to familiarise them with the patterns of literary language. Read to children and discuss the author's intention, the language used and the effect on the listener. Also discuss the main features that provide the audience with enough information to enjoy the story. Where did it happen? Who are the characters and what are they like? When did this story take place? This will assist children to make the transition from recounts of personal experiences to a more mature narrative form with a recognised structure.
- Explore different reading models and demonstrate that they can have different styles.
- Refer to environmental print.
- Read a variety of texts to children. Provide ample opportunity to discuss fiction and non-fiction material.
- Use narrative and informational texts to enhance children's understanding about sequence, procedures, text structure etc. Pictures and picture books provide great stimuli for language use.
- Use shared books for cloze activities to help children predict the language pattern using syntactic, graphophonic or semantic cues.
- Retell stories from a story map.

Teaching Emphases

Use Modelled and Shared Reading to expose children to:

- the joy of reading
- strategies readers use
- print concepts, e.g. that a word is made up of letters
- graphophonic relationships, e.g. initial letters, letters from a child's name, common letter patterns, rhyming words
- common sight words
- print conventions and terminology, e.g. title, content, sentence, paragraph.

Concepts and Conventions

(See p. 37)

Children in this phase need to develop their understanding of the way print is organised. They also need to have a stable concept of a letter and a word in order to move on in writing. It is necessary to give children many opportunities to see and hear correct language patterns so they can continue to develop understandings of the language system.

Use modelled and shared writing to draw attention to various concepts and conventions of print. Allow children time each day for independent writing when they can practise and refine their understandings. Conduct shared reading activities each day. Activities should be tailored to meet current needs. For instance, the need to discuss the use of full stops or capital letters could be a teaching focus for the whole class, small groups or individuals.

Concepts

The following activities may be used to develop children's concept of a word.

- Point to and say each word as it is written on the blackboard or chart.
- Use big books with predictable texts to provide opportunities for text innovation, substitution and word play.
- After reading a large print book several times, cover some of the words and have children predict the words as they arise; use sticky labels that can be removed as children watch and check their predictions.
- Provide opportunities for children to play with words and rearrange words to make different sentences.
- Give oral and written directions to children. Write secret messages on the board and encourage children to decode them and respond to the messages. Give children word and picture cards to build their own messages; in the early stages it may be helpful to use a combination of word and picture instructions.
- Place a variety of functional and informational texts in the reading corner and use these with the children to find information as the need arises, e.g. telephone books, directories, atlases, dictionaries.
- Use language programs such as Bridge Reading to enhance word awareness and develop vocabulary knowledge where appropriate.
- Write a sentence and read it several times with the children. Rewrite the sentence, omitting the last word. Read the remaining words with the children. Repeat this process until all words have been deleted.

- Build up a bank of words frequently written by children. Display and refer to them when appropriate. Encourage children to refer to them when they are writing.
- Use computer programs that will help develop concepts of print.
- Use concept keyboards to enable children to compose stories quickly as they do not have to contend with other aspects of writing such as spelling and handwriting. The writing can be printed in a form similar to that of books. Texts can be illustrated and taken home for further reading. Some children like to have their writing included in the class library.
- Have a computer readily available for children to use. Provide software with programs that children can use. Use computer programs as follow-up activities to consolidate new understandings.
- Encourage small groups of children to use the concept keyboard independently. Have an alphabet overlay or pictures and matching words with simple editing commands for use with the concept keyboard.

The following activities may be used to help children develop the concept of a letter.

- Display an alphabet chart and talk about letters in other contexts, making sure the children can see that a letter is different from a word.
- Make alphabet wall charts cooperatively with children. Display these for reference.
- Use word bank cards as a basis for sorting games. Have children sort the cards into groups using different criteria, e.g. the same beginning letter, end sound, number of letters, long words, short words etc. This will help children focus on particular aspects of words, letters and sounds.
- Combine sounds, letters and whole words on a concept keyboard overlay.
- Make available letters of the alphabet, for children to use and manipulate.

Conventions

Language conventions include spelling, punctuation and grammar. They are the non-negotiable aspects of language and while it is important that children problem solve and puzzle-out their understandings, it is equally important that they have exposure to good models of language. Activities that focus on language patterns should be repeated often.

Punctuation

In this phase it is important for children to notice commonly used punctuation marks that occur in print. Teachers could refer to them incidentally during shared reading and modelled writing.

As they begin to notice punctuation, children may overgeneralise or overuse particular marks; teachers should view this as a positive sign of development.

Teaching suggestions
- Help children develop an awareness of the purpose of punctuation in different contexts.
- Provide opportunities for children to experiment with punctuation marks.
- Incidentally refer to capital letters, full stops, commas or apostrophes as they arise in text.
- Model use of common punctuation marks and talk about their function.

Grammar

Children, particularly those for whom English is a second language, may need constant repetition of conventional language patterns that highlight such elements as subject-verb agreement, noun-pronoun agreement, plurals, word order and so on. They need to understand how sentences are constructed. Conventions of language should be dealt with in context. Shared books or language experience writing and talking provide many opportunities for these activities.

The following activities can be adapted to be used as oral, written or reading activities.
- 'Add one more'
  The teacher gives the singular nouns and children provide the plurals. For example:

one dog	two dogs
one bird	two birds
one church	two churches
one match	two matches
one sheep	two sheep.

  Children build up a collection of singular and plural words, and then try to generalise a rule about how plurals are formed.

- 'Sentence frames'
  These provide children with an enjoyable way to acquire knowledge of conventional language patterns. For example:

I like ...	A fire engine is red
I like ...	A post box is red
I like ...	Apples are red
but I like ... best of all	Bananas are not red.

  The frames can be varied by children or teacher.
- Text innovation
  Use books with simple language structures that allow children to substitute and manipulate words while retaining the familiar language patterns.
- Computers
  Programs that enhance the children's writing process provide a catalyst for writers who may see the whole process of writing as tedious and unrewarding, although they have many ideas they wish to express. If touch-sensitive boards (concept keyboards) are available, an overlay can be designed with pictures. When the picture is touched, the corresponding word appears on the screen. Overlays may also contain words as well as picture cues to enable children to construct their own sentences.
- Simple adventure games on a computer. Discuss events, predict outcomes, draw maps, write related stories etc.

Spelling

Children in this phase may be semi-phonetic or phonetic spellers.

Awareness of sound sequences and phonemic segments of words enhances children's spelling ability. Activities to help develop these skills should be conducted in a meaningful context.

If children are using letter-name spelling, they have come a long way. They have begun to develop a 'system'. Their writing can be read by others and this alone is very encouraging for the beginning writer. They have made the letter-to-sound connection but have not yet worked out the other complexities. Teachers should be very supportive of children's efforts and focus on the message, not just the spelling.

Activities may be used to help children as they develop understandings about the relationship between sound and symbol. Focus on what children know about spelling. Accept and praise approximations and help them to identify sounds in the words.

Teaching suggestions
- Shared-book activities emphasising the sounds of language, e.g. rhyming activities, words with the same first or last sound.

- Games that encourage children to focus on the sounds of words.
- Sorting and classifying words to discover the sounds represented by single letters and letter clusters.
- Using children's names in activities. Have children write their names and identify and name each letter.

Teaching Emphases

These suggestions are to help children develop understanding that:

- the message is in the print
- messages can be written
- print carries a constant message
- writing is arranged left to right, top to bottom
- a word is a unit of print with space on either side
- a word consists of letters
- terms such as word, letter, capital letter, sentence have particular meanings
- punctuation is used in written texts
- written texts are composed in sentences
- a letter can represent a range of sounds
- a sound can be represented by different letters
- access to lists of high frequency words can assist their writing.

Strategies and Attitudes

(See p.37)

- Share feelings about writing.
- Encourage children to start personal journals.
- Encourage children to respond positively to the writing of others.
- Value children's writing attempts.
- Work collaboratively to help students use the 'Things I Can Do' checklist in this book (pp. 113–119).
- Model processes of thinking about writing for instance, 'I need a better word for said. What could I use?'
- Model strategies for spelling words, e.g. 'Does that look right? I'll say the word slowly and make sure I've written all the sounds.'
- Display and provide opportunities for sharing children's writing.
- During modelled writing sessions, record items children have discovered about writing, and assemble to make books for children's future reference, e.g. Things We Know About Punctuation.

Teaching Emphases

In this phase children need to be encouraged to:

- recognise the importance of having-a-go at writing
- use their knowledge of the sound-symbol system to help them write words
- use environmental print, word banks, books and other sources to find words they need to write
- use talk to help make decisions about what to write
- use own experiences as a source of writing
- retell stories and events to order their thinking before writing
- share their writing with others
- give and receive feedback about their written message
- believe that they can be successful writers
- reflect on the things they can do

For Parents

How can I help my child with writing?

- Read to children and encourage them to join in.
- Talk about books before you read them and encourage children to guess what might happen in the story. Sometimes point to particular words or leave words for children to predict.
- Build up a collection of favourite books and read them often.
- Take children to the library to select own books. Don't worry if they choose books which seem too hard — read to or with them.
- Write messages to children and encourage them to write replies. Talk about letters, words, spaces, as you write, e.g. 'Mm... Does that word look right? I'll write it again to see... I'll leave a space here before I write the next word.'
- Use a family message board and encourage children to write their own messages.
- Sometimes try written conversations with children. The idea is to provide a good model without criticising a child's attempts and to encourage children to continue writing, e.g.
  Parent writes: *What did you do today?*
  Child replies: *I plad in the avecha plagron*
  Parent writes: *What did you play in the adventure playground?*
  Child replies: *I plad munkees*
  Parent writes: *What did the monkeys' play?*
- Support children's spelling attempts and praise children's willingness to have-a-go.
- Provide a special place for children to write. Equipment such as a small table or desk and a notice board for displaying writing materials such as scrap paper (lined, coloured or plain), used greeting cards, textas, pencils, pens, envelopes and little note-books would provide an excellent environment for children to experiment with writing.
- Encourage children to make greeting cards for special occasions.
- Talk about the purposes for which you use writing and the advantages of using writing, e.g. telephone messages, recipes or shopping lists to aid memory.
- Use scrap books or books made from spare paper to make personalised books with children. Glue a photograph or picture chosen by children into the book and ask children to tell something about the picture. Let them see you write their words and sentences and use for reading. Add more pages and encourage children to read 'their' book.

- Make an alphabet book with children. As children express an interest in particular words help them to enter words on the appropriate page and keep for children's use as a personal word bank.
- Draw children's attention to a variety of print forms such as telephone books, T.V. guides, magazines, street directories and bank stationery.
- Play games making words from plastic or magnetic letters. Discuss similarities and differences in the way words sound or look. Answer children's questions about print.
- Play games using letter names and sounds, e.g. 'I spy with my little eye'.

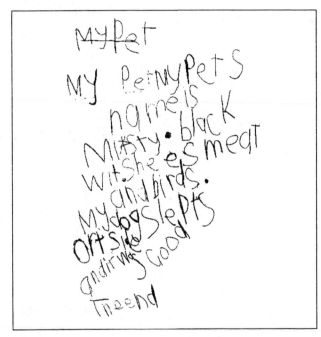

My pet
My pet's name is
Misty. black white.
She eats meat and birds
My dog sleeps outside and
it was good. The end.

Olivia read this to the teacher and looked puzzled when she came to the word 'black'. She said 'I wrote 'she is' in my head. I didn't really leave it out.' Olivia knows a lot about writing.

She is displaying all Key Indicators from the Experimental Phase and some indicators from Early Writing.

Experimental writers have a lot to think about. Praise their efforts.

Early Writing

Children write about topics which are personally significant. They are beginning to consider audience needs. They have a sense of sentence but may only be able to deal with one or two elements of writing at one time, e.g. spelling but not punctuation.

Once in the galaxy far far away there lived a martian. There were a giant he liked eating people. And one day the martian wanted to have a fight with the giant. So he got his shield and, sword

And they had a fight the martian got him in the tummy and the giant was so mad that the mountains shook. He was still alive the martian couldn't believe his eyes so he stabbed him in his tummy again the martian couldn't believe his eyes again

> the Jinte did'nt like this
> blud was dripping from
> histummy He was verry
> mad. He crashed the
> mountains and the houses
> he was so mad the martch
> h was tricky the Jinte
> was facing the his backen
> the marshan sothemarsha
> n stabed him in the back the Jinte

the giant didn't like this blood was dripping from his tummy. He was very mad. He crashed the mountains and the houses he was so mad the martian was tricky the giant was facing his back on the martian so the martian stabbed him in the back the giant

> went oopooowl!!!
> he was sox mad that he
> stamed his right foot
> so hard that the hole
> intire wor*ld broke like
> an egg c*racking. And every
> thing was floating even me.

went ooooow!!! he was so mad that he stamped his right foot so hard that the whole entire world broke like an egg cracking. And everything was floating even me.

Michael's writing shows that he understands how stories are written. His style shows evidence of 'personal voice'. For example:
'He was so mad that he stamped his right foot so hard that the whole entire world broke like an egg cracking. And every thing was floating, even me.'
◆ **uses a small range of familiar text forms (narrative)**
◆ **chooses topics that are personally significant**
• uses a partial organisational framework, e.g. simple orientation and story development
• is beginning to use some narrative structure
• is beginning to use 'book' language (Once in a galaxy far far away ...)

• attempts to transfer knowledge of text structure to writing
◆ **uses basic sentence structures and varies sentence beginnings**
◆ **can explain in context, some of the purposes of using writing, e.g. shopping list or telephone message to aid memory**
◆ **experiments with words drawn from language experience activities, literature, media and oral language of peers and others**
◆ **begins to develop editing skills**
◆ **attempts to use some punctuation**
• rereads own writing to maintain word sequence

Early Writing Indicators

(See also Phase 3 Phonetic Spelling and Phase 4 Transitional Spelling of *Spelling: Developmental Continuum*)

Content, Organisation and Contextual Understandings

(See p. 61)

The writer:

- ◆ **uses a small range of familiar text forms**
- ◆ **chooses topics that are personally significant**
- ◆ **uses basic sentence structures and varies sentence beginnings**
- ◆ **can explain in context, some of the purposes of using writing, e.g. shopping list or telephone messages as a memory aid**
- uses a partial organisational framework, e.g. simple orientation and story development
- often writes a simple recount of personal events or observations and comments
- uses time order to sequence and organise writing
- is beginning to use some narrative structure
- is beginning to use some informational text structures, e.g. recipes, factual description
- writes simple factual accounts with little elaboration
- includes irrelevant detail in 'dawn-to-dark' recounts
- attempts to orient, or create a context for the reader, but may assume a shared context
- rewrites known stories in sequence
- includes detail in written retell
- includes several items of information about a topic
- is beginning to use 'book' language, e.g. 'By the fire sat a cat'.
- joins simple sentences (often overusing the same connectors, e.g. 'and', 'then')
- uses knowledge of rhyme, rhythm and repetition in writing
- repeats familiar patterns, e.g. 'In the jungle I saw ...'

Word Usage

(See p. 65)

The writer:

- ◆ **experiments with words drawn from language experience activites, literature, media and oral language of peers and others**
- discusses word formations and meanings; noticing similarities and differences
- transfers words encountered in talk, or reading, to writing
- highlights words for emphasis, e.g. BIG.

Editing

(See p. 67)

The writer:

- ◆ **begins to develop editing skills**
- deletes words to clarify meaning
- adds words to clarify meaning
- begins to proof read for spelling errors
- responds to requests for clarification
- attempts the use of a proof-reading guide constructed jointly by students and teacher.

Language Conventions

(See p. 68)

The writer:

- ◆ **attempts to use some punctuation**
- sometimes uses full stops
- sometimes uses a capital letter to start a sentence
- uses capital letters for names
- attempts use of question marks
- attempts use of exclamation marks
- sometimes uses apostrophes for contractions
- overgeneralises use of print conventions, e.g. overuse of apostrophes, full stops, dashes and commas
- often writes in the first person
- attempts writing in both first and third person
- usually uses appropriate subject/verb agreements
- usually maintains consistent tense
- writes a title which reflects content.

Strategies

(See p. 71)

The writer:

- ◆ **talks with others to plan and revise own writing**
- re-reads own writing to maintain word sequence
- attempts to transfer knowledge of text structure to writing, e.g. imitates form of a familiar big book
- shares ideas for writing with peers or teacher
- participates in group brainstorming activities to elicit ideas and information before writing
- in consultation with teacher, sets personal goals for writing development
- discusses proof-reading strategies with peers and teacher and attempts to use them in context.

Attitude

(See p. 71)

The writer:

• perseveres to complete writing tasks.

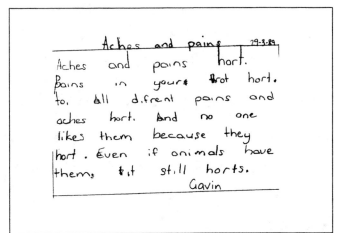

Last Sunday I went to the rollerdrome for my party. and I did some speed skating and when it was finished it was formal skating and before it shut I were skating and I fell over and roller skates rolled over my finger and had to get an x-ray and fractured my bone

Aches and Pains
Aches and pains hurt. Pains in your throat hurt too. All different pains and aches hurt. And no one likes them because they hurt even if animals have them it still hurts.
Gavin

Spelling Indicators

The Key Indicators from the First Steps *Spelling: Developmental Continuum* have been included because learning to spell is part of learning to communicate in written language. For further information about children's spelling development, see the First Steps *Spelling: Developmental Continuum*.

Children in the Early Writing Phase may be in the Semi-Phonetic, Phonetic or Transitional Spelling Phase.

Phonetic Spelling Phase

In this phase, children are able to provide an almost perfect match between letters and sounds. Letters are chosen on the basis of sound, often without regard for conventional letter patterns. Spelling attempts are meaningful and becoming more like standard spelling.

Key Indicators

The writer:

◆ **chooses letters on the basis of sound without regard for conventional spelling patterns, e.g. vampia (vampire), pepl (people)**
◆ **sounds out and represents all substantial sounds in a word, e.g. kitn (kitten), wacht (watched), anothe (another), aftrwoods (afterwards), siclon (cyclone)**
◆ **develops particular spellings for certain sounds often using self-formulated rules, e.g. becoz (because)/woz (was)**

Transitional Spelling Phase

(from sounds to structures)

In this phase, children are moving away from a heavy reliance on the phonetic strategy towards the use of visual and meaning-based strategies. They may still have difficulty recognising if a word 'looks right', but should be able to proof their known bank of words. Writing will show evidence of an increasing bank of learned words.

Key Indicators

The writer:

◆ **uses letters to represent all vowel and consonant sounds in a word, placing vowels in every syllable, e.g. holaday (holiday), gramous (grandma's), honeted (hunted)**
◆ **is beginning to use visual strategies such as knowledge of common letter patterns and critical features of words, e.g. silent letters, double letters**

Robert's letter:

Robert
Dear Mrs Leach
On Saturday my Dad
made me a bow and
arrow and I hit the
target real hard From
Robert

Robert is a Phonetic speller.

Strategies Used by Children

In this phase, children are using some known words and some approximations in their efforts to 'get on' with writing. They also begin to use correct sentence structure and often make generalisations about spelling and print conventions. Their writing resembles 'talk written down'. Some writing may be stilted and 'safe', indicating that the writer is unwilling to take risks. Children should be encouraged to experiment with different forms of writing for different purposes and audiences.

Environmental Print

Children may copy words and phrases. This strategy may be appropriate at times, but should not be the only strategy used.

Repetition

Children may seek sanctuary in the repetition of a particular subject or theme. This is evident when every story is about dinosaurs, trucks, aliens, etc. The characters may change names but the topics are similar. This coping strategy may be used while the child concentrates on other elements of writing.

Talk

Collaborative talk before, during and after writing provides writers with opportunities to plan, clarify and review writing.

Some children constantly seek information from teachers. Teachers need to decide whether to provide this information directly or encourage the child to try alternative strategies and develop independent problem-solving techniques.

Invented Spelling

Most children at this stage have a bank of words they can spell accurately. Children usually include all significant sounds of words, although there may be some unconventional vowel and digraph spelling. They are also beginning to use the visual features of words, as well as the sounds, in their attempts to spell correctly.

Room 8 Wednesday

Dear Ellena
I like you. Do you like me?
I am six. Are you too?
Tomorrow can you play
with me? Do you love
Y.B.? Have you got brown
hair? My favourite colour is
pink. Is your favourite
colour is pink.

Love Amanda

P.S. Do you like Mrs Van
Dyle

P.S. Next is time to take BB
home.

Teaching Notes

Children need to recognise that *function*, *purpose* and *audience* are the major factors influencing their writing choices.

The teacher's role is an enabling and supporting one which encourages children to enjoy writing in a range of contexts. During this phase, continue to model writing and reading each day. It is important to model a large variety of forms of text for different purposes and audiences. During reading sessions, planned opportunities will enable children to develop the ability to 'read as writers' by examining features that make books interesting, discussing what the author needed to know before writing, and looking at text structure and language features. Attention drawn to rhyme, rhythm, repetition, onomatopoeia and alliteration used for special effects in literature, will encourage children to transfer knowledge from reading to writing.

Children need time to interact with their peers and as many adults as possible. It is from this interaction that they will reassess their theories and refine their skills as they move towards more competent, correct and satisfying writing. The type of interaction teachers have with children is critical.

There should be time for children to share with the class or group. During sharing time, children should be encouraged to give a progress report or share a finished product. They may wish to ask for ideas or talk about any writing problems they are facing. Sharing time will allow children to develop understandings of audience needs and adjust their writing according to responses. It is important that children are encouraged to take responsibility for their own learning. Teachers can foster children's self-evaluation by planning for reflection time and by encouraging children to set personal goals for writing.

Major Teaching Emphases

- ◆ **develop an awareness that writing is purposeful**
- ◆ **talk about the differences between oral and written language**
- ◆ **read, write and discuss a range of different forms of writing for different purposes and audiences**
- ◆ **teach planning and revision strategies**
- ◆ **show how sentences are linked to form a cohesive paragraph**
- ◆ **show how paragraphs are linked to form a whole text**
- ◆ **teach strategies for learning to spell new words**
- ◆ **continue to help children develop word banks using topic or theme words**
- ◆ **discuss the selection of words to enhance meaning**
- ◆ **model the use of appropriate linking words**
- ◆ **introduce a proof-reading guide and encourage children to use it**
- • show how titles, headings and other organisational markers can be used
- • allow time for students to explore writing and reading independently
- • allow time for sharing children's writing

- encourage the use of a range of dictionaries and other word sources
- encourage children to set goals and take responsibility for their own writing development

At all phases:

- ◆ **model good English language use**
- ◆ **model writing every day**
- ◆ **encourage students to reflect on their understandings, gradually building a complete picture of written language structures**
- ◆ **ensure that students have opportunities to write for a variety of audiences and purposes**
- ◆ **encourage students to share their writing experiences.**

◆ *Entries in bold are considered critical to the children's further development*

Establishing an Environment for Language Learning

It is important that teachers establish a learning environment that provides opportunities for children to use language (both oral and written) in a variety of meaningful contexts for real purposes. Language is not learned or used in isolation; it is the medium in which we think and work in all areas of the curriculum. The quality of language produced will be directly related to the way teachers and children work together to solve real problems. Teachers need to encourage children to develop enough skills and strategies to work independently in a supportive and cooperative atmosphere. Children therefore need to feel comfortable about taking risks as they tackle new problems. Time should be set aside to enable children to share their writing and discuss any problems they have encountered. Children are still coming to terms with the complex task of writing and they may regress in a specific area while concentrating on a different aspect of the writing task.

Ways to Create an Environment for Language Learning

- Plan writing experiences across the curriculum to enrich children's language knowledge and provide a shared context for spoken and written activities to follow.
- Publish children's writing for a real audience.
- Set up a class library that contains a variety of reading materials both commercially produced and produced by class members.
- Work with children to provide a print-rich environment reflecting the needs and interests of the class.
- Display and refer children to words commonly used in writing.
- Make available a range of dictionaries and other word sources.
- Make sure an interesting range of writing materials is easily accessible to children.
- Use a problem-solving approach to teaching new forms of text.
- Present a range of reading materials to support the writing program. Select texts that display good models of the particular text type being taught.
- Encourage and praise attempts at spelling.
- Encourage children to aim for conventional spelling (especially of frequently used words).
- Ensure that cooperative learning is encouraged by allowing for flexible grouping of children.
- Give children time for personal writing.
- Plan opportunities for peer tutoring.
- Allow children sufficient time to practise new skills.

Content, Organisation and Contextual Understandings

(See p. 54)

Many children have now developed a bank of personal words they can use confidently. They require more strategies to develop ideas fully and to organise their writing to suit different audiences and purposes. Opportunities to talk will complement the reading and writing program. Children need to write expressively about topics they choose and require guidance to help them use writing to entertain, to inform or to persuade. Strategies to extract and organise information should also be included in a varied program.

The *Writing: Resource Book* provides strategies and suggestions for introducing a range of written forms.

Modelled and Shared Writing

Modelled writing can be used to demonstrate the processes and products of writing. The teacher 'thinks aloud' while writing for the audience of children and shows how writers make selections about what to write and how to write. The focus is chosen to suit the needs of the audience. In this phase, children need to see how different texts are planned and constructed. Modelled writing sessions can be conducted for the whole class or for small groups of children who have particular needs. When introducing something new, teachers may need to model the process many times before attempting shared writing sessions and eventually encouraging children to practise the skill in independent writing.

The following suggestions can be adapted to suit specific needs.

- Model how to choose a topic
  Brainstorm and record suggestions. Include a range of ideas that requires the use of different forms of text. Some suggestions may be:
      a thank you letter; the recipe I promised my aunt; a project about my hobbies; a big book for the preschool children; a class serial.
  Categorise suggested topics and keep notes for use in later modelled writing sessions.
- Model selection of detail
  Children in this phase may need help to select essential detail to make their writing interesting and to understand what the reader needs to know. Their writing seems to 'ramble on'. Show how to focus or refine information by modelling. On large sheets of paper, prepare or model the writing of a recount which includes irrelevant detail.

Read the text to the children and discuss what is wrong with it, e.g. the beginning is boring, it includes unnecessary detail. Talk about the need to keep the attention of the reader and to include information that will be helpful, but not distracting, to the reader. Put a line through any details which are not essential. Ask children to suggest ways to make the beginning more interesting. Revise and refine the recount. Make use of children's writing samples to demonstrate this process.

- Model forms of writing
  Writing may be modelled in a variety of different contexts. Selection of forms depends on purpose for writing.
  Model writing in all curriculum areas, including social studies, health, mathematics and science.
  Model unfamiliar forms of text and encourage children to discover the specific features of that form, e.g. a friendly letter requires the address of the sender, a greeting, some information, a suitable salutation and the address of the recipient. If any one of these components is missing, the letter will not achieve its goal. In using the problem-solving approach, children will be able to choose the necessary framework and language features for their writing and then evaluate its success. Chart children's 'rules' for writing each form and keep the chart as a reference for future writing.
      Suggested range of texts:
      – recounts
      – procedures or instructions
      – descriptions
      – simple reports
      – summaries
      – letters
      – invitations
      – greetings
      – narrative forms

– poetic forms
– lists
– written or oral retells

Shared writing gives children the opportunity to see demonstrations, participate and practise before they are expected to write independently.

Take every opportunity to talk with children about their ideas, feelings and experiences. This will assist children to clarify their thoughts and order their ideas.

The following suggestions for shared writing can be adapted for use in oral language and reading.

- Teacher and children jointly construct a form of writing. Discuss the way in which the text is structured and the type of language appropriate for that form.
- Make use of writing in all subject areas to record activities or information with children. For instance, record the processes used in mathematics to give children an opportunity to clarify and review their maths understanding while writing.
- Pair an older child with a younger child and have them work collaboratively on a piece of writing, ensuring that both children participate.
- Label and write sentences about interesting things inside and outside the classroom, e.g. the adventure playground, the new computer, the dog with three legs.
- Jointly construct, display and use various forms of functional print, e.g. timetables, calendars, rosters, class rules, word charts and so on.
- Record class events as a wall story or recount. Write a serial together accepting some suggestions from children.
- Read a factual text with children and jointly construct a written or oral retell that contains the important information.

The writing program should include opportunities for children to write, read and discuss a range of narrative and expository texts.

Narrative writing suggestions

- Make a Choice
  Conduct 'choose your own' adventure story activities. After reading a range of adventure stories, teacher and children compose two (or more) alternatives for each section of the story, e.g. setting, characters, actions and reactions, quests or complications, resolutions. Children then choose a path to follow and compose their own adventure story. Compare adventures and make a class book of adventure stories.
  This activity can be adapted for use with other types of narratives, such as fables, myths, science fiction etc.

- Take a Chance
  This activity will help children compose a story by providing ideas for some elements of a narrative. Make three sets of ideas cards (use different colours). On one set, write ideas for settings, e.g. the ocean, the jungle, a haunted house. On the second set, write ideas for characters, e.g. the giant, a small girl, a robber. On the third set, write ideas for problems or complications, e.g. a missing diamond, a violent storm, a flooded river, a bloodstained carpet.
  Children work in groups and one child selects a card from each set of ideas cards. Group members discuss the possibilities and make up a story orally using the suggestions from the cards. Children then attempt to write their own stories (these may vary from the group story). Encourage writers to add extra elements and elaborate details of the story-line.

- Changes
  Children take a known story and rewrite it, changing one or more elements. For example, they may change the setting, the main character or the ending.

- Sequencing
  Place pictures in a sequence and orally tell a story. Write the story.
  Sort sentences into sequence to make a story.
  Rearrange jumbled sentences to make a story.
  Order paragraphs to make a story.

- Oral Story Telling
  Retell known stories.
  Tell stories from key words given by teacher.
  Tell stories from pictures.

- Describe a Character
  Children vote for a class citizen of the week. The child chosen draws a self-portrait while the remainder of the class writes a sentence or paragraph describing some positive character traits displayed by the person. The portrait and written statements are displayed and then given to the citizen.

Expository writing suggestions

- Classification
  Brainstorm what children already know about the chosen topic. Record all suggestions. Discuss ways to classify or categorise information into sections. Use these categories as headings to plan writing and reading. Make a list of questions to guide research. Research and take notes to record additional information needed to complete the writing task. Use the headings as a writing plan and add further details.

For example:

Bears

Type	Where found	What it looks like	Food	Other information
Polar				
Brown				
Grizzly				
Panda				

- Questions
  Children work in groups to compile a set of questions from a non-fiction text they have read. Groups swap questions and write answers, paraphrasing from the text but trying to write in the same style.

Teaching Emphases

In this phase use modelled and shared writing to help children develop understanding that:

- the purpose and audience dictate the form which writing takes

- successful writing is writing that achieves its purpose

- a range of different texts are planned and constructed differently, e.g. stories, recounts, procedures, exposition, reports

- texts have different styles and language features

- there are certain reader expectations of texts, e.g. a story is expected to entertain, a report is expected to inform, a procedure is expected to provide instructions

- writers need sufficient knowledge of the topic to write successfully and direct experiences are only one source of writing

- a reader's interpretation of a text is enhanced if the writer includes relevant contextual information

- writers make selections about how and what to write

- writing may need to be modified if it is to be read by others

- writing can be used to communicate over time and distance, e.g. messages, direct experiences or feelings.

Independent Writing

Teaching suggestions

- Give students opportunities for personal choice writing. Diaries and journals allow children to tackle the problems of written language and use writing as a means of self-expression. The teacher may need to be careful to respect the child's right to privacy and only read personal writing if invited to do so.

- Provide opportunities for children to write recounts of class experiences, reports in science or social studies, recipes, directions, rhymes, limericks, poetry, letters, invitations, advertisements for coming class events, stories, journals and diaries, maths procedures and explanations, notes for projects or any other purposeful writing.

- Encourage children to use a journal to respond in writing after various learning experiences, e.g. after maths ask children to write 'What did I find out today' and 'What I am still not sure about'.

- Encourage children to write for purposes they see as relevant to them, e.g.
  – a letter to a television station to ask that a popular program be rescheduled to a more convenient time
  – a guide for visitors to the school
  – a play script from a favourite story to perform for an audience
  – a recipe to try at home
  – instructions for a game.

- Provide planning sheets to assist children when they are learning new forms of writing. See First Steps *Writing: Resource Book* for suggested frameworks.

Planning Frameworks

RECOUNT PLAN

TOPIC:

1. SETTING: WHO? WHERE? WHEN? WHAT? WHY?

2. EVENTS IN TIME ORDER
Event 1
Event 2
Event 3
Event 4

3. CONCLUDING STATEMENT/ENDING

Sample planning sheet from 'Writing: Resource Book'

Sample planning sheets from 'Writing: Resource Book'

NARRATIVE PLAN

NAME: DATE:

TITLE:

ORIENTATION:
Setting: Who? When? Where? What? Why?

INITIATING EVENT
What began the event? How did the characters get involved?

COMPLICATION/S:
How the conflict/s or problem/s began

RESOLUTION:
How the character/s solve the conflict/s or problem/s.

Modelled and Shared Reading

Teaching suggestions

Read and write with children every day and provide quality literature models. Discuss the language and structures used by various authors. Talk about the processes and strategies used by good readers as they read.

- Demonstrate different approaches used when reading factual and narrative texts. Show children that these are read in different ways because the purpose for reading is not the same, e.g. factual texts can be used to locate specific information without reading the entire text. Narrative text has a storyline and needs to be read through to follow the plot.
- Cover the headings in an informational text and ask children to write suitable headings, after reading the relevant text.
- Read a variety of texts. Select material from all areas of the curriculum to demonstrate forms of writing. Show attitudes to particular texts, e.g. curiosity, delight, amazement.
- Invite children to comment on the different styles of writing they encounter.
- Read a short story or novel to children, stopping before the end. Ask children to suggest several possible endings. Continue reading and compare the author's ending with those suggested by the children. Discuss which endings were the best.
- Invite children to identify and comment on bias or inconsistencies in texts.
- Help children get started in writing by reading a number of opening sentences from books and talking about the ways in which authors entice readers to continue reading.
- Encourage children to think about and discuss various aspects of reading that may influence their writing.
  What do we know about the author?
  What did the author need to know to write this?
  How has the author tried to make you think?

How has the author portrayed the main character?
Are there any things about the character that you like/dislike?
Do you know anyone who is like the character?
Do the words the character says tell you anything about him/her?
Could you draw or describe the character?
How has the author tried to make you dislike a character?
How does the author help you to 'see' things that are in the book? Choose some of your favourite phrases and write them in your journal. Illustrate the phrase to show your mind-picture.

Independent Reading

- Have an attractive book corner that is easily accessible to children and frequently introduce new material.
- Provide an area where children can be comfortable as they read.
- Try to build on children's interests by acquiring extra books by favourite authors or about popular topics.
- Provide a range of written material in different genres.
- Create an environment that is rich in functional print, e.g. labels, signs, charts of known songs and poems, helper's rosters, instructions for use of equipment.
- Provide access to taped stories with accompanying texts.
- Encourage children to publish material and leave it for others to read.
- Show children how they may choose books and allow time every day for uninterrupted reading.
- Actively promote new reading material as it becomes available.
- Draw attention to and encourage the use of labels and signs in the classroom and outside.
- Encourage children to keep a personal reading log in which they enter titles of books read and any comments that they feel are relevant. Sometimes use the log as a focus for reading conferences.

Word Usage

(See p. 54)

Children need to be encouraged to extend their vocabulary and use words that convey more precise meaning to the reader. Teachers should provide interesting and varied activities to make children aware of alternative words which may be used to clarify meaning. Shared and modelled reading sessions provide ideal opportunities to introduce and discuss new vocabulary.

Use modelled and shared writing to demonstrate how to choose and use vocabulary that is precise. Discuss different words with similar meanings and selections made for a particular piece of writing. Allow time for independent writing so that children can refine and practise using new vocabulary. Make available charts or alphabetical lists that feature essential new vocabulary and refer to these charts throughout the day.

The following activities enable children to use and refine new vocabulary.

- Retelling favourite stories (both orally and in writing). This activity allows children to practise the use of new vocabulary from literature without having to think about inventing a new story-line.

- 'Noun Describers (or String Poems)'
  Materials required are blank cards, a pin-up board and felt pens.

  Decide on the topic, e.g. puppies. Have one or two children prepare at least twelve cards with the topic word (puppies) on each. Discuss how puppies feel, look, sound and play. Place three of the 'puppies' cards across the top of the pin-up board.

  As children suggest an adjective describing puppies write it on a card and place the card on the pin-up board for all to read. Place three descriptive words on each line and then add the word 'puppies' to the end of each line. Read each line as it is pinned-up and re-read all previous lines. Keep adding cards and re-reading. When there are sufficient (six or eight lines of words describing puppies) place the last three 'puppies' cards across to make the last line.

  This activity provides a chart that can be used for individual or group reading. Children rearrange the words to improve the rhythm, sound or sense. Provide copies for children. Leave the cards where children can rearrange them. After a time, collect cards and place them in an envelope marked 'Puppies' or chart them for children's reference.

This chart was developed by a Year 2 class.

Puppies			
Puppies	puppies	puppies	
cute	cuddly	playful	puppies
fat	fluffly	friendly	puppies
bouncing	biting	awkward	puppies
snapping	yapping	barking	puppies
hungry	thirsty	panting	puppies
puppies	puppies	puppies	

- Classifying and Sorting
  In the context of art and craft provide a range of materials for children to sort and classify using their own criteria. Encourage children to describe the attributes of articles in each group. Model the use of descriptive language, e.g. 'All of these nails are sharp and shiny. Those are bent and rusty'.

- Who Am I?
  After reading several stories, ask children to choose a character they wish to describe. Children make up clues to describe the character's appearance or personality. These clues are written on one side of a card. The name of the character is placed on the reverse side. The cards may then be used in group guessing games. It is important to focus children's attention on the type of details to include in their descriptions.

- Make an Animal
  Children work in groups. Each child writes an adjective on a piece of paper. After discussion, papers are

arranged in an appropriate order. Children then draw an object featuring all attributes listed and write the description, e.g. a large, angry, prickly, shiny bird. The pages can be collated to make a 'Strange Animal' book for the class library.

- Subject-specific Vocabulary
  In areas such as social studies, science and health there are opportunities to introduce new or interesting words, e.g. social studies — The Community. Brainstorm to find public facilities available in the community.

What is it?	Who works there?	What do they do?
School Library Shire Council Hospital Shops		

Each group selects a facility and finds relevant information. The information may be presented to the class. Discussions and questions should follow each presentation so that children have time to internalise new vocabulary. The finished charts could be used as a focus for making comparisons or for further investigations.

- Literary Devices
  During shared reading or writing sessions, draw attention to rhyme, rhythm, repetition, onomatopoeia and alliteration used for special effects.

- Word Classification
  Use a selection of words from any subject area, e.g. social studies, and classify the words under headings such as food, shelter and clothing. Justify selection.

- Words and Pictures
  Start with a word you wish children to remember and have children find pictures that portray that word to them. Encourage children to discuss their pictures with peers.

- Card Games
  Children prepare two sets of cards, one colour for each set. On one set, write words from personal lists or other sources. On the other set, write matching definitions. Use the cards to play Concentration, Snap, Fish or Rummy.

- Word Association or Semantic Maps
  Start with any word. Children take turns to nominate another word that is associated in some way. The associated word may rhyme, have the same meaning or be related in another way. Children may be asked to explain their choice of words.

- Multiple Meanings
  Compile charts using words with more than one meaning, e.g. bank — money bank; a river bank; a bank of clouds; the aeroplane banked suddenly; a Blood Bank; cars banked up at the traffic lights.

- Prefixes and Suffixes and Other Endings
  Children compose a paragraph containing a number of words that require a prefix or suffix or other ending and give to partner as a cloze exercise, e.g. I was _ _happy and _ _ _appointed because I had miss_ _ the final episode of my favourite show. I'_ been watching this show for three month_ and was look_ _ _ forward to see_ _ _ what happen_ _ to the hero.

- Tired Words
  Children choose overused words from their own and other people's writing and then use a thesaurus to find alternative words.

- Compound Words
  Prepare a set of cards that, when placed together, could form compound words. Children play Concentration, trying to accumulate as many compound words as possible.

Encourage children to use environmental print.

Editing

(See p. 54)

Children need to be taught explicitly how to revise and edit their writing. Children in this phase will probably be able to add or delete words, but may have difficulty reordering words or parts of text. Teachers need to demonstrate or model the sort of behaviours they expect of children and talk about the process as they model. It will take time and practice for children to become competent at these skills. It is advisable to start with short pieces of writing and concentrate on one or two revising or editing skills.

It may be useful to work with children to devise a checklist they can use independently later.

Sample checklists

Revising	
Clarity	*Do I understand this writing? (Mark places where meaning isn't clear.)*
Anything left out	*Have I included all necessary information for the reader?*
Sequence	*Could the ideas be placed in a better order? How?*
Unnecessary information	*Is there any information that could be left out?*

Editing	
Punctuation	*Does the punctuation help to make the meaning clear?*
Paragraphing	*Do any of the ideas need a new paragraph?*
Spelling	*Have I checked the spelling? (Underline any words that cause concern.)*
Sentences	*Are there any sentences that could be simplified or which need elaboration?*

Encourage children to work with peers to use the checklist to modify their writing.

Proof Reading

- Use a piece of draft writing from a child of similar age to those being taught. Duplicate the piece so that each child has a copy. Revise and edit the piece together. Children make alterations on their copies. Discuss and justify all alterations.

- Sometimes type a child's writing and have children revise and edit the typed copy.
- Encourage children to read and re-read their writing aloud to check that it makes sense.
- Arrange partner conferences. Train children to edit each other's writing cooperatively.
- Teach children to read their writing and identify words they wish to improve or words that have been overused. Encourage discussion of these words to assist children to find substitutions which will improve writing.
- In shared writing sessions, guide the class or group in composing, revising, editing and publishing a piece of writing from start to finish.
- Encourage children to use editing facilities on word processing software.

Teaching Emphases

Use modelled and shared writing sessions to demonstrate techniques for:

- changing what has been written
- re-reading to check for meaning
- what to do if a mistake is made
- crossing out words
- inserting words
- rearranging words or pieces of text
- checking available sources for correct spelling
- starting again if the writing is unsatisfactory
- underlining words that may be spelled incorrectly
- attempting the spelling of new words.

Language Conventions

(See p. 54)

In this phase of their development, children have a good concept of a word and a letter. They need to develop the concept of a sentence and to use language structures and punctuation that help clarify the meaning of written language. It is also necessary for them to become aware of the differences between oral and written language.

Written language conventions include punctuation, grammar, spelling and conventions associated with particular forms of text. They are important aspects of the language and while it is important that children problem solve and puzzle-out their understandings, it is equally important that they are exposed to good models. Modelled writing and shared reading provide opportunities to draw attention to print conventions in context. Activities that focus on language patterns should be repeated often.

Teaching suggestions
- Use modelled and shared writing and reading to draw attention to the differences between oral and written language.
- Allow children time each day for independent writing so they can practise new skills and refine their understandings.

Punctuation

Teaching punctuation in a meaningful context, using a problem-solving approach, is far more effective than asking children simply to punctuate a piece of unrelated text from a book of exercises. Use samples of children's own writing, texts from shared reading or modelled writing to teach the use of punctuation in context. It may be appropriate to have whole-class, small-group or individual instruction, depending on the needs of the children.

Children need to understand that punctuation is used to clarify meaning and to help the reader know how the writing is meant to sound when it is read aloud.

The following problem-solving approach to teaching the use of capital letters may be adapted to teach the use of other conventions, e.g. full stops, question marks or quotation marks.
- Select a known big book (meaningful context) that uses a range of capital letters for different purposes, e.g. to begin a sentence, for names of people and places, days or months etc.
- Ask children to find the words with capital letters and group them into categories according to their function.

- In small groups, children then work out a set of rules for using capitals (problem solving).
- Discuss their findings.
- Look for other capital letters. Discuss function and reason for use.
- Make a chart of children's rules for using capitals and leave space for any additional rules that may need to be added.

- Direct Speech
  Many writers in this phase begin to include direct speech in their writing and may need help with punctuation. The following strategy may be useful as an introductory activity.

  Rewrite a piece of text containing direct speech. Use a different colour for the direct speech of each character. Read the text, noting where the quotation marks are used to open and close speech. Choose children to role play the characters, only reading the direct speech. Discuss the placement of the quotation marks and have children work out some guidelines for punctuating direct speech, e.g. a comma before opening speech marks, a full stop to show that the speaker has finished. Children work in groups to test and refine their punctuation theories by referring to other examples in different texts.

Grammar

It is important that children understand the way our language system works. Most people who speak English as a first language understand and use many conventions of grammar because they have been surrounded with the structures of the language all their lives. They may not be able to articulate rules or name parts of speech but they are conscious of what sounds *right* and what does not. Second-language speakers may have difficulty with English language structures and need more practice to refine their understandings and come to terms with the system of language, or the grammar, in order to express meaning clearly.

As with punctuation, grammar should be taught in a context that is meaningful to children. It should be taught at the point of need. This may mean whole-class, small-group or individual teaching.

Some problems typical of writing in this phase are:
* failure to relate pronouns to their antecedents. *The man hit the boy and he yelled loudly. Then he got into trouble ...*
* overuse of 'and then' to connect phrases or clauses. *We went out and then we had dinner and then I watched TV and then I went to bed.*
* difficulty with inflectional endings -s, ed, ing (this problem is particularly common with children for whom English is a second language).

These problems can be dealt with by modelling correct usage orally and in writing. It may be necessary to conduct group or individual conferences. Teachers should respond to the message first and accept that children may be using a home language. The transition to standard English, although desirable, may take time.

The following activities provide opportunities for children to play with language and practise skills that will help their understanding of the language system and common language structures.

* Inflectional Endings
  Use a designated base word. Ask children to think of as many endings as they can for that word. The new words must be real words. Use the dictionary to check. Discuss the changes of meaning. For example:

ring	*ride*
rings	*rides*
ringing	*riding*
ringer	*rider*
ringed	

* What a Change!
  Use a sentence from a child's writing, e.g. 'Last week I swam at the beach'.
  Discuss alternative phrases for 'Last week' and list the suggestions underneath.
  Next discuss alternatives for 'I' and list those. Continue in this way until each part of the sentence has been considered.

Last week	*I*	*swam*	*at the beach.*
In summer	*he*	*played*	*in the pool.*
Yesterday	*they*	*jumped*	*in the lake.*

Children then choose one phrase from each column to make a sentence.
Tense changes and subject–verb agreements may be discussed as they arise.

* Play with Sentences just for Fun
  Ask children to make sentences in which each word begins with the same letter. Sentences may be nonsensical, but they must be grammatically correct, e.g. Ants and antelopes are always angry.

* Work on 'Stretch a Sentence' Activities
  Children work in groups of five or six. Teacher writes a short sentence or phrase, providing a copy for each group. Each group member adds one word to make the sentence more interesting or informative. Share each group's sentence and encourage children to comment on the merits of each.

The following activities are suggested to help children recognise the differences between oral and written language.

* Oral Sentence Combining
  Practise combining one, two or three sentences.
  For example: *The boy is big.*
  He has a blue hat.
  He plays football with his sister.
  These sentences can be combined in many different ways and any combination which makes sense and retains meaning should be accepted, e.g. *The big boy, with the blue hat, plays football with his sister.*

* Expanding Sentences
  Start with a simple sentence and expand it by adding a word, phrase or clause.
  For example:

The	boy ran home	
troubled		*to tell his mum*
sad		*after his fall*
naughty		*before he was hit*

* Discuss sentences as 'units of meaning'. Help children develop a concept of 'sentence'. Model sentences on the board.

* Provide time for children to work with sentences taken from their writing. Children cut these sentences into words and reconstruct the sentences in different ways.

* Try stressing different words in a sentence such as 'You are leaving tomorrow' to show how this alters the meaning. Discuss how intonation and stress could be conveyed in written form.
  For example:
  '*You* are leaving tomorrow.'
  'You *are* leaving tomorrow.'
  'You are *leaving* tomorrow.'

* Choose a piece of writing from a novel or story you are going to read. Put a section on an overhead transparency, deleting all nouns, adjectives or verbs.

Have children suggest possible replacements. Write them in the appropriate spaces. Read the original text. Compare children's suggestions with the original and discuss the similarities or differences. Talk about why particular words were chosen.

- Introduce topic sentences as the main idea of a paragraph. Teach children to develop paragraphs that contain information related to the topic sentence.
- Before children begin a piece of writing, have them illustrate each new idea or part of the piece. Each new picture could be the start of a new paragraph.
- Introduce a number of sentences about aspects of a social studies or science topic that has been covered. Ask students to work in groups to compose a paragraph using the given sentence. Discuss how students add supporting details to support the topic sentence.

Spelling

As children develop their language skills, they will make approximations of adult spelling. Accept that these approximations are a positive sign of development and teach children strategies for learning to spell new words. Children should be encouraged to focus on the way a word looks and to look for patterns and relationships in words.

Provide models of, and discuss spelling strategies. Encourage children to talk with peers and adults about their writing and the spelling of unknown words.

Teachers should engage children in the following activities:

- What Comes Next?
  This game is played in the same way as 'Hang-the-Man', except that the letters must be given in order and only one letter is recorded at a time. This gives children the opportunity to use their knowledge to predict the letter patterns that are likely to appear. It is essential that a copy of the alphabet is made available for the children's reference. Focus on 'demon' words and words which can not be sounded out, but which have predictable letter sequences, e.g. enough.

- Card Games
  Card games such as Concentration, Happy Families, Fish, and Snap can be adapted for use in spelling activities, e.g. find a pair of words containing the same sound but different spelling, such as 'eat' and 'been', or the same spelling but different sounds, such as 'head' and 'bead'.

- Have-a-Go pad
  Children use a 'pad' of scrap paper to have-a-go at spelling words used in writing. They think about significant features of the word and write it several times to arrive at the best possible approximation. They choose the word that looks right. Their efforts should be praised.

Teaching Emphases

These suggestions are to help children develop understanding that:

- written and oral language are constructed differently and are used for different purposes
- written texts rely on punctuation, selection of precise descriptive words and text structure to enhance meaning
- written texts need to be explicit and include contextual details to assist the reader to construct meaning
- conventional spelling is essential when writing is to be published
- written language is organised into sentences and paragraphs
- paragraphs contain information about one aspect of a topic
- paragraphs are linked to form a cohesive whole text.

Strategies and Attitudes

(See pp. 54–5)

- Encourage children to prepare for sharing time by brainstorming suggestions about the conduct of sharing sessions. Make a chart with their suggestions listed, e.g.

> **When I share my writing I:**
> - Make sure I am well prepared
> - Consider my audience
> - Ask for suggestions to help me improve my writing
> - Thank people for their help
> - Think carefully about the suggestions
> - Make some decisions about my writing.

- Engage children in evaluating their own writing.
- Work with children to set goals for writing. Talk to children about the type of writing they might do in the next two or three weeks. Chart the suggestions. Discuss what children may need to learn about writing in that period and establish short-term class goals. Negotiate specific goals with children and include details about the topic, intended audience, purpose, form of text and publishing details.

The following goals were negotiated in a Year 4 class:

> **Writing suggestions**
> - a letter
> - a poem
> - a ghost story
> - a report about snails
> - notes for projects

> **Class Goals**
> - a published piece of writing
> - learn how to set out a letter
> - practise note-taking

> **Personal goals**
> I will:
> - write a poem about my new puppy
> - publish it and read it to the Year 1 class
> - write a letter to Grandma

- Encourage children to monitor aspects of their writing development in their journals, e.g.
  I use capital letters:
    to begin sentences
    for names of places and people
    for days and months
    for titles and special days.
  I use the following punctuation correctly:
    full stops
    commas to separate items in a list
    question marks
    apostrophes to join words, e.g. I'm.
  I write sentences.
  I use joining words that make my writing more interesting.
  I have a go at spelling first and then check if I'm not sure.
  Before I write I think about:
    why I am writing
    my audience
    my writing plan.
  As I write I read and re-read my work to see if it makes sense.
  After I write I:
    see if I can improve my writing
    ask someone to help me with revising and editing
    publish my writing in appropriate and suitable ways to achieve my purpose.
- Invite children to work in pairs or groups to help each other improve their writing
- After a number of writing demonstrations, children will be able to offer suggestions for improving a piece of writing. Encourage children to work in collaborative groups to brainstorm suggestions for improvement. Chart suggestions for future reference, e.g.

> **When I write a story I:**
> - Get ideas down first
> - Make sure the beginning is interesting
> - Include interesting characters
> - Include dialogue to move the story along or give information about character's personality
> - Read it to a friend and ask for suggestions
> - Check for spelling and punctuation.

Teaching Emphases

- Encourage children to brainstorm, share ideas and talk about their writing to activate their background knowledge before they start to write.
- To help ascertain which details should be included in their written text, encourage children to think of the needs of their intended audience by imagining that they are in that role, or asking others to assume the audience role and asking questions.
- Invite children to use planning sheets to organise information or to provide a guide for independent research.
- Include sharing time so that children can give and receive feedback.

For Parents

How can I help my child with writing?

- Praise children's writing efforts and respond to the message rather than the grammar or spelling. Prominently display children's writing and demonstrate that you enjoy and value children's writing.
- Have fun writing messages to each other. Try writing reminders, riddles and secret messages.
- Look for opportunities for purposeful writing activities at home. Adults and children can write notes, telephone messages, holiday plans, helper's rosters, greeting cards, letters to friends or to relevant places for information.
- Start a family diary to record special days, funny sayings, weekend activities and other significant events. Include photos, letters cards or other mementos relevant to family. Share reading of the journal with family members.
- Talk with children to help them clarify their thinking about their writing.
- Talk with children about the sort of writing they are doing at school. If you are involved in writing for work show children how you write and explain why you are writing.
- Encourage children to use a word processor or typewriter if one is available.

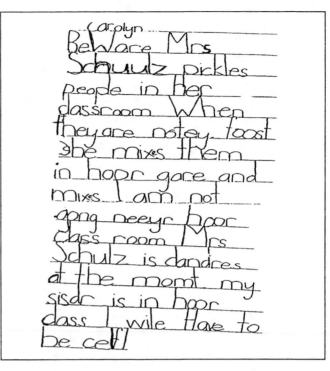

Beware
Beware Mrs Shulz pickles people in her classroom.
When they are naughty first she mixes them in her jar and mixes. I am not going near her classroom. Mrs Shulz is dangerous at the moment my sister is in her class I will have to be careful.

- Read children's draft writing and comment on the things you like about it. Encourage children to figure out their own answers, e.g. have-a-go at spelling a new word and then use a dictionary to check. Provide help if children ask for it but leave final decisions about writing to the writer.
- If your children ask you to help them 'fix' their writing for publication or for a project, check with the teacher to see if children are using an editing checklist at school and obtain a copy. Work cooperatively with children using the list.
  The following list may be helpful. Read the writing aloud.
  - Can I understand this writing? (Mark any places where the meaning isn't clear)
  - Could the ideas be placed in a better order?
  - Are there any details that could be left out?
  - Does the writing achieve the purpose for which it was written?
  - Have I checked that the punctuation helps to make the meaning clearer?
  - Have I checked the spelling? (Underline any words that cause concern)

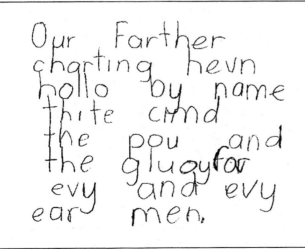

Our Father which art in heaven
Hallowed by thy name
Thy Kingdom come
The power and the glory
For Ever and Ever
Amen

- Read to your children every day. Vary the type of material you read. Include interesting newspaper articles, factual books as well as stories, poems and rhymes. Make reading to your children a special quiet time when you can enjoy the experience.
- Give presents that encourage reading and writing. These could include a range of books to read, notebooks, diaries, envelopes, attractive writing paper, pens, coloured felt pens and so on.
- Make sure children have access to a dictionary that they can use. There are simple picture dictionaries and 'Junior' dictionaries available.
- Involve children in purposeful reading activities such as reading recipes or directions. Assist children with unfamiliar words but give children time to have-a-go and praise their efforts. Involve children in collecting and writing favourite recipes for the family recipe book.

- Play word games from magazines and newspapers and commercial games such as 'Scrabble', 'Boggle' and so on.
- Try simple crossword puzzles and 'Find the Word' puzzles.
- If children have access to a computer, have a program which involves them in writing or spelling for real purposes, rather than one which simply drills spelling out of context, e.g. solving puzzles, making or completing crosswords, choose your own adventure games.

Early writers need time to talk about their ideas and may need help to make plans.

PHASE 4 Conventional Writing

Writers are familiar with most aspects of the writing process and are able to select forms to suit different purposes. Their control of punctuation, spelling and structure may vary according to the complexity of the writing task.

HOW THE SPIKEY GECKO GOT ITS SPIKES

Long ago in the Simpson Desert, way back in the Dream Time when man was not settled yet, lived the Gecko. Only one though. One day in the cool of the afternoon, layed Neera the Gecko. Her long smooth body curled on a rock laying peacefully in the afternoon sun. All the other lizards were jealous of Neeras lovely smoothe skin. That night, while all was asleep, there was a rustle! Then a thump! All the animals were awakened by this noise. They stood in total amazement, there standing in the moonlight was a man, with a kangaroo skin covering below, and a spear. He had dark complexion, and no one had seen anything like it before! The animals ran and hid. And Neera stood there with her googly eyes staring, and her head moving side to side in amazement. The man took a step towards Neera, she wasn't really expecting this, so she shot up a tree.

The next morning the man was nowhere in sight. Later on that day Neera found the man hunting in a bees nest. (Looking for honey) Neera made everyone like the man, and from this day on everything has gone smoothly. Until………one day all the animals were out hunting for tonights dinner, so was Neera. She was looking flies and mozzies to cook for herself and the fat frog next door who was to lazy to hunt for himself. Anyway, while hunting she was walking along not doing a thing to anyone, when suddenly AAAAAAAAAAAAHHHHH!!!!!!! Neera had slipped into one of the mans traps. Neera felt another spike go into her as she rolled over. After all that she got up and as Neera got up she noticed her reflection in the pond, and she had spikes along her back. Neeras eyes bulged as she saw the unique and unusual spikes along her back. Now she was one of a kind. That night all the animals had a feast, nobody cared about Neeras spikes they were happy that she was the most original animal in the Dreamtime.

From this sample we can assume that the writer:

- ◆ **uses text forms to suit purpose and audience**
- takes account of some aspects of context, purpose and audience
- establishes place, time and situation
- demonstrates the ability to develop a topic
- demonstrates knowledge of differences between narrative and informational text when writing
- is developing a personal style of writing
- ◆ **uses a variety of simple, compound and extended sentences**
- ◆ **is beginning to select vocabulary according to the demands of audience and purpose, e.g. uses subject-specific vocabulary**

- includes specific vocabulary to explain or describe
- edits and proof reads own writing after composing
- ◆ **punctuates simple sentences correctly**
- organises paragraphs logically
- ◆ **uses a range of strategies for planning, revising and publishing own written texts**
- uses knowledge of other texts as models for writing
- ◆ **groups sentences containing related information into paragraphs**

Conventional Writing Indicators

(See also Phase 3 Phonetic Spelling, Phase 4 Transitional Spelling and Phase 5 Independent Spelling of *Spelling: Developmental Continuum*)

Content, Organisation and Contextual Understandings

(See p. 83)

The writer:

- ◆ **uses text forms to suit purpose and audience**
- ◆ **can explain why some text forms may be more appropriate than others to achieve a specific purpose**
- ◆ **writes a range of text forms including stories, reports, procedures and expositions**
- ◆ **uses a variety of simple, compound and extended sentences**
- ◆ **groups sentences containing related information into paragraphs**
- takes account of some aspects of context, purpose and audience
- considers the needs of audience and includes background information
- uses rhyme, rhythm and repetition for effect (where appropriate)
- demonstrates the ability to develop a topic
- demonstrates knowledge of differences between narrative and informational text when writing
- organises the structure of writing more effectively, e.g. uses headings, sub headings
- can write from another's point of view
- shows evidence of personal voice (where appropriate)
- is developing a personal style of writing
- establishes place, time and situation
- often includes dialogue
- uses dialogue to enhance character development
- shows evidence of the transfer of literary language from reading to writing
- organises paragraphs logically
- uses titles and headings appropriately
- orders ideas in time order or other sequences such as priority order
- uses a variety of linking words such as *and, so, because, if, next, after, before, first.*

Word Usage

(See p. 88)

The writer:

- ◆ **is beginning to select vocabulary according to the demands of audience and purpose, e.g. uses subject-specific vocabulary**

- uses some similes or metaphors in an attempt to enhance meaning
- varies vocabulary for interest
- includes specific vocabulary to explain or describe, e.g. appropriate adjectives
- uses adverbs and adjectives to enhance meaning
- uses simple colloquialisms and clichés.

Editing

(See p. 90)

The writer:

- ◆ **uses proof-reading guide or checklist to edit own or peers' writing**
- edits and proof reads own writing after composing
- reorders text to clarify meaning, e.g. moves words, phrases and clauses
- reorders words to clarify meaning
- attempts to correct punctuation
- recognises most misspelled words and attempts corrections.

Language Conventions

(See p. 91)

The writer:

- ◆ **punctuates simple sentences correctly**
- uses capital letters for proper nouns
- uses capital letters to start sentences
- uses capital letters for titles
- uses full stops to end sentences
- uses question marks correctly
- sometimes uses commas
- uses apostrophes for possession
- uses apostrophes for contractions
- writes effectively in both first and third person
- uses appropriate subject-verb agreements
- uses appropriate noun-pronoun agreements
- maintains appropriate tense throughout text

Strategies

(See p. 93)

The writer:

- ◆ **uses a range of strategies for planning, revising and publishing own written texts**
- selects relevant information from a variety of sources before writing

- can transfer information from reading to writing, e.g. takes notes for project
- brainstorms to elicit ideas and information before writing
- attempts to organise ideas before writing
- plans writing using notes, lists or diagrams or other relevant information
- sets and monitors goals for writing
- uses knowledge of other texts as models for writing
- re-reads and revises while composing.

Attitude

(See p. 93)

The writer:

- writes for enjoyment
- writes to get things done
- experiments with calligraphy, graphics and different formats
- manipulates language for fun, e.g. puns, symbolic character or placenames (Ms Chalk, the teacher, Pitsville).

How the Galah Became Pink and Gray

Long ago in the land of Wonga there lived an artist who had many different colours. His paints didn't come off things. All the birds, including the white galah, watched the artist paint. He painted the butterflies wings and he painted sculptures of padducks and meadows. One day while flying around the white galah was wondering how he could get some pretty colours like the butterfly. The white galah went to ask the king and queen fairy of the forest if he could get permission off the artist to paint him yellow and purple. They said no because they thought that the animals and birds should stay the colour they there. The poor white galah went back home and was sad, so he went to bed. He got out of bed and went outside. An eagle tried to get him by swooping down and clawing the galah. The galah just kept running forwards instead of going back to his house. He accidentally ran into the gray and pink paint the artist had left outside. It tipped all over the white galah and the galah became pink and gray. The artist was angry because the galah had ruined his beautiful paint, but the galah was happy because he wasn't white any longer. That's how we see the galah today with its beatiful pink and gray feathers

A lovely tale ~ well told too!
Well done!

Spelling Indicators

The key indicators from the First Steps *Spelling: Developmental Continuum* have been included because learning to spell is part of learning to communicate in written language. For further information about children's spelling development, see the First Steps *Spelling: Developmental Continuum*.
Children in the Conventional Writing Phase may be in the Phonetic, Transitional or Independent Spelling Phase.

Phonetic Spelling Phase

In this phase, children are able to provide an almost perfect match between letters and sounds. Letters are chosen on the basis of sound, often without regard for conventional letter patterns. Spelling attempts are meaningful and becoming more like standard spelling.

Key Indicators

The writer:

◆ **chooses letters on the basis of sound without regard for conventional spelling patterns, e.g. vampia (vampire), pepl (people)**
◆ **sounds out and represents all the essential sounds in a word, e.g. ktn (kitten), wacht (watched), spidr (spider), isgrem (ice cream)**
◆ **develops particular spellings for certain sounds often using self-formulated rules, e.g. becoz (because)/woz (was)**

Transitional Spelling Phase

(from sounds to structures)

In this phase, children are moving away from a heavy reliance on the phonetic strategy towards the use of visual and meaning-based strategies. They may still have difficulty recognising if a word 'looks right', but should be able to proof their known bank of words. Writing will show evidence of an increasing bank of known words.

Key Indicators

The writer:

◆ **uses letters to represent all vowel and consonant sounds in a word, placing vowels in every syllable, e.g. holaday (holiday), gramous (grandma's), castel (castle), replyd (replied), gorrilas (gorillas)**
◆ **is beginning to use visual strategies, such as knowledge of common letter patterns and critical features of words, e.g. silent letters, double letters.**

Independent Spelling Phase

In this phase, children have become aware of the many patterns and rules that are characteristic of our spelling system. When spelling a new word they use a multi-strategy approach. They have the ability to recognise when a word doesn't look right and to think of alternative spellings. Spellers in this phase will have accumulated a large bank of known words they can automatically recall.

See *Spelling: Developmental Continuum* or page 99 of this book for indicators.

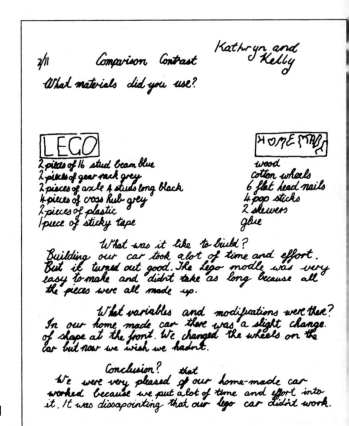

Strategies Used by Writers

In this phase, children are beginning to deal with all elements of the writing process. As they address a new skill, there may be regression in other areas. For instance, if there has been an emphasis placed on punctuation, some children may regress in their use of correct spelling or sentence structure until they have internalised the use of punctuation. It is important that teachers recognise these regressions as temporary. During this phase of development, understandings and skills are consolidated and expanded.

Environmental Print

The writer uses words and ideas from many sources and seeks specific words or phrases to fulfil his/her needs at the time. Wall charts, reference books, stories read, signs and other sources are all consulted. This strategy is used by older writers and demonstrates that they have a purpose, a problem to solve and are taking responsibility for their own learning. These factors are significant in the development of writing.

Repetition

Children may write frequently about the same topic, e.g. favourite TV programs. This decreases the need for children to focus on creativity and provides an opportunity for them to concentrate on other aspects of writing. A topic chosen by a child may elicit approval and interest from teachers and peers. This may lead to whole-class interest in writing about the same topic, e.g. 'monster' stories, 'science fiction' stories.

Talk

Writers continue to interact with peers and adults to clarify ideas and receive feedback on their efforts. This process is crucial for the development of writing.

Invented Spelling

At this stage there is less emphasis on phonetic spelling and more emphasis on the appearance of the word. Children cope with spelling by:
- transferring their acquired knowledge to assist their attempts with unfamiliar spelling, e.g. l *ight*, br *ight*
- using a dictionary
- selecting a different word that they can spell
- writing a word indistinctly in such a way that the reader has to deduce what is meant.

I don't think it's a very good idea to put the hotel there because:

Nature Reserve
The nature reserve could be a tourist attraction, but the roads would get busier and the animals could get run over on the road. Also the animal could get scared of the noise and the people that tour there could try to touch them. The tourists could also try to pick the flowers there too.

Industrial Estate
The industrial estate wouldn't be a very nice site to see, and if you were on the opposite side in the hotel to the beach you would out your window and see the industrial estate. The industrial site causes pollution too, and the air would smell!

Airport
The airport has good and bad points to it. The planes would fly over the hotel and make alot of noise; but the hotel isn't very far from the airport, and it wouldn't be very far to get from it to the hotel

Writing in different contexts requires writers to extend their knowledge of written forms.

Teaching Notes

Although children in this phase have acquired more knowledge of written language, they will continue to benefit from daily modelling of reading and writing behaviours. Children are becoming familiar with most aspects of the writing process and are beginning to select appropriate forms of text to suit different purposes. It is vital that children have a clear understanding of the purpose and the intended audience for writing. If either of these essential elements is not clear to the children, their writing will stagnate. Teachers need to provide a variety of contexts for writing to extend children's knowledge of written forms.

Teach children how different texts are structured and used for different purposes in various contexts. Construct frameworks with children as a starting point for writing a new form of text. Allow children time to practise and then help them to evaluate their written work using the framework as a guide for discussion. For example, *'Let's look at our Report framework and see how our reports match our framework guidelines. You organised these reports well but there are still a few things to learn about the type of language required for a report. Let's see if we can find some reports in books and look at the type of words used'.*

Encourage children to talk about their writing and to take responsibility for improving it.

Continue reading aloud daily to enable children to appreciate patterns, rhythms and nuances of language. Provide a reading and oral language program to complement writing, and include a wide variety of forms of text in all areas of the curriculum.

Major Teaching Emphases

◆ **teach children to plan and write both narrative and informational texts**
◆ **help children to adapt their writing to suit the intended purpose and to explore alternative ways of expressing ideas**
◆ **discuss linguistic features of basic text types**
◆ **teach children appropriate use of organisational markers such as topic sentences, paragraphs and headings**
◆ **show different ways of linking paragraphs to form a whole text**
◆ **encourage the use of a variety of linking words**
◆ **encourage children to take responsibility for their own learning**
◆ **teach revising, editing and proof-reading skills**
◆ **discuss and foster 'personal voice' and individual style in writing**
◆ **teach children the conventions of language (punctuation, grammar and spelling) in context**
• provide meaningful contexts to analyse and teach forms of text
• help children increase their oral and written vocabulary
• teach strategies for learning to spell new words and encourage children to increase their personal word lists
• provide examples that show the structure of written texts and talk about ways to improve written texts

At all phases:

◆ model good English language use
◆ model writing every day
◆ encourage students to reflect on their understandings, gradually building a complete picture of written language structures
◆ ensure that students have opportunities to write for a variety of audiences and purposes
◆ encourage students to share their writing experiences.

◆ *Entries in bold are considered critical to the children's further development*

Establishing an Environment for Language Learning

Language is not learned or used in isolation; it is the medium in which we think and work in all areas of the curriculum. The quality of language produced will be related directly to the way teachers and children work together to solve real problems for real reasons. Teachers need to encourage children to develop enough skills and knowledge to work independently in a supportive and cooperative atmosphere where they feel comfortable about taking risks as they tackle new problems. The school program ought to be balanced and interesting, so as to promote writing as an enjoyable and useful activity.

Ways to Create an Environment for Language Learning

- Work with children to provide a print-rich environment that reflects the needs and interests of the class; as new aspects of writing are covered, jointly construct reference charts so children know where they can retrieve information at a later date.
- Display children's writing alongside commercial publications.
- Promote a community of writers within the classroom.
- Establish interest centres where children may select writing activities to do.
- Organise and plan activities that require children to work independently.
- Involve children in setting their own writing goals and goals for whole-class writing activities.
- Publish children's writing for a real audience.
- Talk about the needs of audience. Allow time for children to share their writing.
- Ask children to adopt an author and see if they can find information about the author's books and life.
- Expose children to a range of quality literature and talk about favourite books and authors. Talk about what authors need to know to write. Discuss how authors are able to attract and hold the attention of the readers.
- Problem solve with children and allow children to formulate rules about language use.
- Model writing each day, including such elements as word selection, use of punctuation, sentence structure, forms of text, how to have-a-go at spelling new words, topic selection, organising information, note-taking, planning strategies and proof reading.
- Enjoy poetry with children and encourage them to read and recite poems so they can feel the rhythm.
- Encourage children to write poetry; start with simple frames of known poems that feature rhyme, rhythm and repetition.

- Introduce different poetic forms such as haiku, cinquains and limericks.
- Read and discuss different types of informational texts in all curriculum areas.
- Encourage an interest in words. Allow children to play with words; do crosswords and work out rules for doing them. Look at word sleuths, palindromes, words inside words, rebus words and other word study activities.
- Encourage and praise all spelling attempts.
- Encourage children to aim for conventional spelling.
- Make available a range of dictionaries and other word sources.

Content, Organisation and Contextual Understandings

(See p. 76)

Writers in this phase have mastered some of the mechanics of writing and are aware of a variety of text forms. They have yet to master all the linguistic and structural features required for composing and organising these texts. Mastery of these skills is best achieved by maintaining links among purpose, audience and form. In addition, writers may need assistance to select information which is likely to be required by potential readers.

Children also need explicit teaching to show the similarities and differences between the structures of oral and written language.

The First Steps *Writing: Resource Book* provides strategies and suggestions for introducing a range of written forms and information to help teachers assess children's progress in writing some forms of text.

Modelled and Shared Writing

Continue to use modelled writing and shared writing to introduce or consolidate important aspects of writing in all curriculum areas. Large sheets of blank paper clipped to an easel provide an ideal medium for demonstrating writing processes and writing products. The text can be retained for future reference or revised at a later date for publication.

Teachers may demonstrate processes and products such as:

- how to write a range of informational and narrative texts
- writing across the curriculum for different purposes and audiences
- how to adapt writing to suit purpose and audience
- the use of organisational markers such as topic sentences, paragraphs and headings
- note-taking strategies
- how to write full sentences and paragraphs using notes or key words from research reading
- topic selection, e.g. list three things you hate doing, three things you like doing, three places you have visited, three people you know, three great things that have happened to you, three awful things that have happened to you and three things you can make. Read the list carefully. Select three or four possible topics for writing. Discuss these. Choose one to write about and leave the list available for future use. Encourage children to copy the procedure for their own writing
- how to lay out or design a book for publication.

- Introducing new forms of writing
Read a variety of texts that are written about the specified topic in the form to be introduced and discuss the way each piece achieves its purpose. Compare the examples and rank them. Consider the organisational framework and other aspects of the text such as tense, language, punctuation etc. With the children, draw up a framework of the key features that are essential to achieve the purpose of the text. During a shared writing session, jointly construct a piece of writing using the framework developed. Display this framework for children's reference. Encourage children to practise writing the selected form independently and to use the organisational framework to evaluate their own writing. Discuss the writing and decide whether or not the purpose has been achieved.
- Jointly construct written retells of fiction and non-fiction texts.
- Text Innovation
Read a text that has a repetitive sequence. In groups, or individually, children write a story trying to retain the same kind of story structure using a different topic or changing some words to alter the meaning.
- Story Maps
Choose stories that have a recognisable plot and trace the story path on a map that shows where the characters went and what happened at each site.
- Read a story that features a number of characters. Build up a pen portrait of each character. Discuss what the author needed to know about these characters and how the author may have found out about the type of characters. Collect pictures of people and have children work in groups to build up pen portraits of each. Share the descriptions with class. Discuss how these characters could be involved in a narrative. Jointly construct a story plan. With the children, construct a narrative using the characters and the story plan. Return to the text, re-read and revise the writing in

front of the children. Plan for publication. Follow-up activities could include letters to the characters, advertisements for actors to play parts in a screenplay version of the story or play script of the story.

- Before commencing the study of a particular topic in science, health or social studies, compile a skeleton outline that includes all information children already know about the topic. After studying the topic, have children use the same framework and insert all additional information discovered. Compare and contrast the two skeleton outlines.

- Picture Cues
  Have children work in groups. Cover the text of a suitable book so only diagrams or pictures are visible. Ask children to write text to match the illustrations. Uncover the text and compare the content of the children's version to that in the text.

- Please Explain
  Children work in groups. Each group has a set topic to explain, for example, *Why we need trees* or *Why dogs make good pets.* Children all contribute information and do any necessary research before presenting their explanations, orally or in writing, to the rest of the class.

The following activities are suggested to help children recognise the differences between oral and written language and to move from 'talk written down' to the use of written language patterns.

- Paraphrasing
  Prepare four or five short sentences about a topic being studied. Children try to retain the message using one sentence only.

- Sentence Reduction
  Select a sentence from a child's writing or from a book and ask children to identify unnecessary words or phrases. Discuss whether the deletions alter the meaning or the style of the writing. The ultimate question is 'What do you think the author would think about the sentence now?'.

- Stretch a Sentence
  Work in groups. Start with a short sentence. Pass the sentence around the group, with each person adding or changing one word to make the sentence more interesting. Share the finished sentences with the whole class and discuss which sentences are most interesting.

- Rearranging words
  Write a sentence. Rearrange the words so that the sentence still makes sense although the order of the words has been changed.

For example:
  Jane came running with her toy train in her hand.
  With her toy train in her hand, Jane came running.
  Jane came, with her toy train in her hand, running.
  Running, with her toy train in her hand, came Jane.
Discuss which sentences 'sound right' and why. Have children talk about which groups of words can be moved together, e.g. *Jane came running* and *with her toy train.* Use the blackboard to model this and encourage children to participate in the process.

- Language Patterns
  Read poems that have cumulative patterns, e.g. *There Was an Old Lady, The House That Jack Built.* Discuss the patterns and encourage children to observe the different patterns that occur in literature. Use some of these patterns during modelled writing sessions. Allow children to try their own versions.
  Discuss the features of other patterns — rhyming couplet, cumulative repetition.

- Cut and Compare
  With children's help jointly compose a written retell of a known tale. Make copies for children and have them cut up sections and match each part with that part of the original story. Compare the language used.

The following activities are designed to help children understand the structure and language features of narrative texts so they can use their knowledge to create their own texts. Most of the activities can be oral or written, or a combination of both. They may be conducted with small groups or adapted for use with the whole class. The activities will also assist children in developing ideas and organising them into cohesive whole texts.

- Character Interviews
  Select one child to role play a character from a known story. Have three or four other children ask the character questions to help build up a character profile.

- Letters
  Children work in pairs and each writes a letter to a story character. They swap letters and write a reply from the character's point of view.

Teaching Emphases

In this phase use modelled and shared writing to help children develop understanding that:

- writing is a thinking process
- writers develop their own style
- the purpose and audience dictate the form which writing takes
- successful writing is writing that achieves its purpose
- writers need sufficient knowledge of the topic to write successfully and direct experiences are only one source of writing
- reading and analysing texts of published authors will help own writing development
- there are certain reader expectations of texts, e.g. a story is expected to entertain, a report is expected to inform, a procedure is expected to provide instructions
- different texts are planned and constructed differently. They have different stages and language features
- planning and organising relevant information before writing will assist the writing process
- written texts need to be explicit and include contextual details to assist the reader to construct meaning
- a reader's interpretation of a text is influenced by background knowledge and cultural differences
- writers make selections about how and what to write
- writing may need to be modified if it is to be read by others
- writing can be used to communicate over time and distance, e.g. messages, direct experiences or feelings.

Independent Writing

- Conduct journal writing activities
  Provide opportunities for daily journal writing and encourage a combination of various forms of journal writing. Teachers can model journal writing by keeping a journal and sharing the contents with the children.
- Suggested journal writing ideas
  Provide opportunities for personal and private journal writing.
  Writing for a response. Teacher responds to the message written. Teachers may wish to designate one group per day for written responses in order to see each journal once a week.
  Writing to learn. Children write about one particular part of the day's activities. This provides an opportunity to clarify understanding.

Writing before and after. Children write all they know about a topic that is to be introduced. On completion of the unit, they write again and compare the two entries.

- Provide opportunities for children to write some of the following forms of text:
  - stories
  - character portraits
  - descriptions
  - poems
  - sets of instructions
  - recipes
  - advertisements
  - expositions
  - slogans and posters
  - friendly and formal letters
  - invitations
  - interview questions
  - arguments from a point of view
  - lists
  - note taking
  - summaries
  - reports
  - recounts
  - jokes, riddles, puns etc.
  - explanations
- Retelling
  Have children read a piece of text and then write it in their own words, retaining the original meaning. Children then work in pairs or groups to read and discuss their writing. Allow children to compare and justify various parts of their retells and then go back to the original text to make further comparisons. Discuss the different language styles and whether or not children used anything from the text or attempted to match their writing styles to the original text.
- Victim or Villain
  This activity helps children to see situations from a different point of view. Read a well known tale and discuss the 'villain', e.g. The wolf in *Red Riding Hood*. Children rewrite the story from the villain's point of view. Compare and share in groups.
- Guess What!
  Children write a few sentences to describe a common object. Partners try to guess what is being described.
- Use opportunities across the curriculum to enable children to practise persuasive writing. For example:
  - Social studies — letters to the council about a new shopping centre near the school
  - Health — the advantages of a healthy diet
  - Literature — writing from the villain's point of view to change the reader's perception
  - Prepare and present debates about relevant issues

- In groups, children discuss their best features. They then write a promotional text about themselves, adding photos or pictures. These may be glued into a scrapbook and titled appropriately, e.g. *Introducing Year Five*.

- Make a Change
Read a traditional tale with children. Discuss what would happen to the story if one aspect was changed, e.g. In *Hansel and Gretel*, if the setting was changed from the woods to a modern city, or the stepmother was kind, or the ending was different. Have children write a new version of a traditional tale, experimenting with changing one aspect.

Modelled and Shared Reading

Plan a reading program that supports writing in the classroom. Engage children in prediction activities when reading to assist their understanding of text structures. If children are required to write a particular style or form of writing, they should have access to a range of published material that demonstrates that form. Shared reading followed by independent reading of the same or similar texts will immerse children in the structures and language used, and this will assist their understanding as they attempt to write using a particular form.

- Story Starts
Using quality literature, read the opening paragraphs and discuss how various authors were able to command the reader's attention.
Begin a chart of favourite opening sentences and add to this as different stories are read. Encourage children to use these in their writing.
This process may help children move away from the predictable use of adverbial or adjectival phrases and clauses of time (e.g. Last week…; Once, long ago…; During the night…).

- Making Comparisons
Select a range of particular types of narratives; for example myths, fairytales or fables. Read and discuss the common features of each, such as setting, characters, complications and resolutions. Make a grid to which children can add information as they read more of the same text types.

For example, a study of fairytales may result in a grid with these headings:

	Story Name		
	Cinderella	Hansel and Gretel	Ugly Duckling
Characters			
Setting			
Problems			
Ending			
Moral/theme			

- Select an Ending
Read many different types of stories and discuss endings used. Select a well-known tale and discuss some possible alternative endings. Children retell another tale and change the ending. Model using a story from a child of similar age and ability. Stop reading before the end of the story. Brainstorm several different endings, making sure that the endings are suited to the plot.
Have children work in groups or pairs to decide on several possible endings for their own stories. Discuss which endings would satisfy the reader best and why this is so. Compile a list of some elements or features that endings should have to satisfy audience requirements.

- Analysing the Plot
Have children list the important events of a known story and then select the most exciting part or the climax.

- Literary Devices
During shared reading sessions discuss the special effects achieved by the use of rhyme, rhythm, repetition, onomatopoeia and alliteration. Discuss the use of imagery, similes and metaphors to enhance meaning by creating vivid word pictures.
When reading with children, discuss how authors use particular devices.
For example: (a) repetition to evoke images of effort and strain
I think I can, I think I can…
They ran and they ran and they ran…
He huffed and he puffed…
(b) figurative language — alliteration, metaphor, onomatopoeia.

- Analyse the Advertisement
  Children examine advertisements in different types of magazines. Discuss how advertisements differ (audience interest). Teacher selects an advertisement and models how it might be modified if it were to appear in a publication that has a different audience, e.g. political journals, teenage magazines, fashion catalogues. Discuss the devices used to attract the reader, the promises made explicitly and the implied advantages. Have children design their own advertisement for a particular purpose and audience.

- Analysing and Writing Advertisements
  Collect advertisements and discuss the use of pictures, print size, language and layout. List all stated benefits and all suggested benefits. Compare the vocabulary in each list. Discuss the persuasive language used and the devices that attract attention. Model the construction of an advertisement. Plan opportunities for children to write advertisements.

Independent Reading

Children's literature provides the hub of a rich language program, so time devoted to independent reading will enable students to see what real writers do. Students need to be encouraged to read as writers and write as readers. Real books provide models for writing and many concepts introduced in shared reading or writing sessions will be consolidated as students return to texts or apply their knowledge and understanding to other texts.

The teacher's role is to provide a variety of literature and to introduce students to many authors and titles. By demonstrating their own love of reading teachers can encourage children not only to learn to read but to choose to read.

Students can be encouraged to keep reading logs that show reading undertaken.

Students need to be able to choose their reading material so that they learn to select books to suit their interests and abilities and don't require the teacher to *make* them read.

Word Usage

(See p. 76)

Teachers need to help children enjoy the richness and variety of words in our language. Immersion in quality literature will assist this development. A variety of word games and investigations will also encourage children to become conscious of word usage in oral and written language.

Teachers who organise fun, problem-solving activities so children can manipulate words and investigate word origins or word meanings, find that children are willing participants who take pride in building up extensive personal word banks. Children will also be more selective in their use of words to create precise meaning.

Use modelled writing and shared writing to demonstrate how to choose and use vocabulary that is precise. Discuss different words with similar meanings and why selections are made for a particular piece of writing. Allow time for independent writing so children can refine and practise using new vocabulary. Make available charts or alphabetical lists that feature essential new vocabulary and incidentally refer to these throughout the day. Shared reading provides opportunities to discuss effective use of various literary devices.

The following activities give children opportunities to use and refine new vocabulary.

- Favourite Words
  After reading a story or poem, have children decide on a word they would like as their own. Write the word on a card and enable children to build up a bank of these words. Allow time to play with the word cards. Encourage activities such as sorting, sentence making, alphabetical order.
  Teacher-directed activities can also be undertaken, e.g. teacher begins a sentence, leaving off the last word, and children try to find a word in their bank that would be a suitable sentence ending. Teacher gives a sentence, leaving out a verb (or adjective, adverb, noun etc.) Children find a word card that will fit correctly. Share all suggestions and discuss.

- Picture Clues
  Children work in groups or with a partner. Have children find pictures from magazines or newspapers. Children then find words that could relate to the picture. Share with other groups and add new words as they are suggested. Leave on display as a reference.

- Word Origins
  Group words with a common root. Discuss meanings and ask children if they can tell what the root means, e.g. *capital, captain, decapitate* from Latin root *caput* meaning *head*. Compose a table displaying the root word, its origin, its meaning and a list of words derived from it.

- Alphabet Roundabout
  Choose a category, e.g. *Words that Describe Food*. Children then try to find a word for each letter of the alphabet which fits the nominated category.

- Crossword Puzzles
  Teach children strategies for solving crossword puzzles. Devise rules to help children solve puzzles. Make use of the *Wesoft* crossword puzzle computer program to compose class puzzles that relate to topics being studied. Allow children to select words and compose clues to make their own puzzles.

- Many Meanings
  Select common words that have many meanings, e.g. *run, bank, out, up, wet*. Have children discover many meanings for the words and then, with a small group, use the words in paragraphs or poems in as many ways as possible. Share the results.

- Draw a Word
  Children choose words from a given word bank and try to write each word in a way to illustrate its meaning, e.g. *hot, tall, shivering, humid, glittering, angry, surprised.*

- Use a Thesaurus
  Choose an entry in the thesaurus. Children then rank the given words in order of intensity, e.g. *amusing, funny, hilarious.*
  Put children in pairs. Choose a word. Give a limited time for children to write as many synonyms as they can. Use a thesaurus to decide the winner.

- Change the Meaning
  Write a sentence stem and have children add a link word and then complete the sentence orally, e.g. *The car will crash*
  > if…
  > when…
  > although…
  > because…
  > but…
  > after…
  > so…

Discuss how the end of the sentence changes when the linking word changes.

- Making the Links
Present a piece of writing with the linking words deleted. From a list of possible words, children insert the most appropriate word for each space. Discuss and justify use of particular words. Discuss the need to use precise linking words to signal the relationship of ideas. List several different linking words and work with children to construct sentences using these as precisely as possible. Discuss the different purposes of words used.

Teach children to use a variety of linking words in appropriate contexts.

Some types of linking words

- cause and effect may be signalled by *if-then, because, so*
- time order may be signalled by *then, subsequently, after that*

- comparisons and contrasts may be signalled by *like, different, from, however, similarly, likewise*
- alternatives may be signalled by *on the other hand, otherwise, or*
- space relationships may be signalled by *under, over, at the left, above, in the foreground*
- different points of view may be signalled by *alternatively, otherwise, nevertheless, conversely, however, on the other hand, on the contrary*
- addition of ideas may be signalled by *likewise, too, again, besides, and further, in the same way*
- reiteration or repetition may be signalled by *that is to say, indeed, in other words, in short, expressed in different terms*
- conclusions or consequences may be signalled *by hence, thus, so, consequently, accordingly, as a result, therefore*

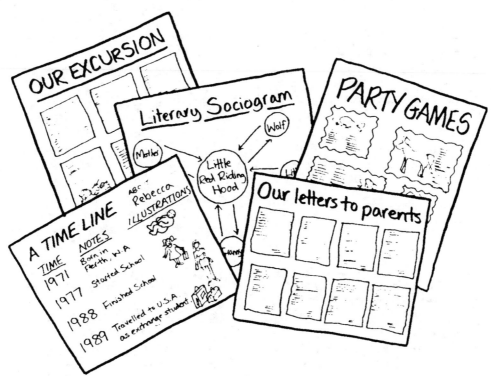

Children must feel that their writing is purposeful, relevant and worth revising.

Editing

(See p. 76)

Children still need explicit teaching to revise and edit their writing. The skills required should be modelled frequently by the teacher. In this phase, children should be able to re-order parts of a text. This skill is easily demonstrated using word processing software designed for use by children. Help children to see that writing is flexible and that feedback from an audience can help an author shape and change a text to achieve more impact.

When revising, editing and proof reading their writing, students need to understand that the purpose is to clarify the meaning of the text.

Encourage students to consider:

- **Audience**
  Is the information accurate and appropriate for the audience?
  Is the language appropriate for the audience?
  Is there enough background information?
  Will the writing achieve the effect intended?
- **Purpose**
  Does the writing achieve the designated purpose or goal?
- **Form**
  Is the chosen form appropriate for purpose and audience?
  Are the conventions of the form evident?

Teachers should work with children to devise a checklist they can use independently.

A sample checklist

- **Revising**

Clarity	*Do I understand this writing? (Mark places where meaning isn't clear)*
Anything left out	*Are there enough details for the reader?*
Sequence	*Could the ideas be placed in a better order? How?*
Unnecessary information	*Is there anything that could be left out?*

- **Editing**

Punctuation	*Does the punctuation help to make the meaning clear?*
Paragraphing	*Do any of the ideas need a new paragraph?*
Spelling	*Have I checked the spelling? (Underline any words that cause concern)*
Sentences	*Are there any sentences that could be simplified or that need elaboration?*

Proof-reading techniques

- Encourage children to proof read their first draft and mark words they wish to improve or words that have been overused. Encourage the use of a thesaurus or the discussion of the words with peers to expand their vocabulary.
- Obtain writing samples from children of the same age group. Demonstrate proof-reading strategies, e.g. using a ruler under the line of text being read; reading the passage backwards; underlining any words that might be wrong. Use both handwritten and typed samples.
- Stand-back technique
  For children who cannot see that their writing is unclear to others, it may be helpful to type the piece with double spacing. Children are then removed from their writing and seem to be able to edit it more critically.
- Word Processing
  Allow children to write using software that offers word processing facilities.

Teaching Emphases

During modelled writing sessions, teachers could demonstrate how they write by:

- selecting particular words for their shades of meaning or suitable sounds
- rearranging pieces of text to improve cohesion or coherence
- inserting or deleting words
- using word processing software
- adding detail to make readers feel part of the action
- underlining words that may be spelled incorrectly
- using appropriate punctuation.

Language Conventions

(See p. 76)

As children extend their repertoire of text forms, they need to understand the use of conventions within these forms. Modelled writing and shared reading can provide meaningful contexts in which teachers can show how these conventions are used. Children need a more extensive knowledge of how to use punctuation marks to clarify meaning. They also need to learn how to make their writing more cohesive by linking sentences into paragraphs and linking paragraphs into a whole text. Conventional spelling is also a desirable goal.

For a range of activities and strategies, see First Steps *Writing: Resource Book.*

Punctuation

The following activities may be used to introduce or consolidate understandings.

* Using Direct Speech
  Many students include direct speech which is difficult for the reader to follow. They need to be able to punctuate accurately so the reader can follow the conversation. They also need to understand that dialogue should add something to the characterisation or the plot of the story.
  The following questions may help improve the quality of dialogue. These should be modelled by the teacher and used in joint compositions so children will use them when they wish to include direct speech in their writing. Ask:

  Is it easy to see who is speaking?
  Does the punctuation help to show how the dialogue should be read?
  Does the dialogue help to reveal the plot?
  Does the dialogue suggest anything about the type of characters who are speaking?
  Would these characters really say this?

  Read many texts that include direct speech and discuss how the author uses speech to give readers insight into characters or plot.
* Punctuating Direct Speech
  Model using a section from a comic on a transparency. Introduce dialogue from the speech bubbles of the comic. Discuss what each character said. Write the conversation as it would appear in a piece of text, adding any extra information needed to clarify the meaning, e.g. *said Tim, shouted Piglet.* Emphasise teaching points such as a new line for each new speaker, where to open the quotation

marks and where to close them etc. Have children work in groups or pairs and then individually to document the speech from different sections of a comic strip. Select a short story or chapter in a novel that has several characters and includes direct speech. Make a copy for groups to work with and have children turn the text into a play script by deleting all except the dialogue and then including a part for a narrator to set the scene or link the spoken parts.

Grammar

Children need to be given language to talk about language. They need to know what the various parts of speech are called so they can talk about words and their function. Teachers should introduce terms such as noun, adjective, adverb and verb to refer to words in context. Children can then problem solve and discuss the function of each. Terms for structure words such as prepositions, pronouns, conjunctions and auxiliary verbs could be introduced when the need arises.

* Parts of speech
  Write a passage of text from a book that has been read. Delete all adjectives. Ask children to substitute words that will retain the sense of the passage.
* Discuss the words used
  Problem solve to find out what function particular words serve and where they are positioned in sentences, for example, find all adjectives in the text. Discuss their function and position in sentences. Ask children to write a definition of adjectives that would be useful for someone who is learning English. This activity could be adapted to teach other parts of speech.

Publishing Conventions

Present a range of texts that illustrate the use of layout, artwork, design and presentation.
Discuss these and encourage children to use the information when they publish their writing.

Conventions of forms of writing

When introducing forms of writing, take care to present conventions of that form.

The layout of some forms is dictated by conventions that do not apply to other forms, e.g. job applications, business letters, graphs, tables, plays and film scripts all have different conventions that are generally accepted as necessary to that form.

Spelling

Provide opportunities for:

- Word sorting activities, enabling students to sort words according to sound, visual and meaning patterns (see *Spelling: Developmental Continuum*, Transitional Spelling Phase, Complementary Activities; and Independent Phase, Complementary Activities and *Spelling: Resource Book*, Chapter 4, Word Study)
- Segmenting and blending using Secret Messages (see *Spelling: Resource Book*, Chapter 3, Teaching Graphophonics)
- Sound Sleuth activities (see *Spelling: Resource Book*, Chapter 3, Teaching Graphophonics)
- Playing with words (see *Spelling: Resource Book*, Chapter 4, Word Study)

Teaching Emphases

These suggestions are designed to help children develop understanding that :

- written and oral language are constructed differently and are used for different purposes
- written texts can be enhanced by use of organisational markers such as topic sentences, paragraphs and headings
- sentences containing information about one aspect of a topic are linked to form a paragraph
- paragraphs are linked to form a whole text
- written texts rely on punctuation, selection of precise descriptive words and text structure to enhance meaning
- conventional use of punctuation, grammar and spelling is desirable.

Strategies and Attitudes

(See pp. 76–7)

- Invite children to use planning sheets to organise information or to provide a guide for independent research.
- Share a range of strategies for planning, revising and publishing written texts.
- Help writers to analyse a range of texts to compare their structure and linguistic features.
- Encourage writers to monitor own progress as a writer by keeping dated records of writing attempted, writing completed and conference proceedings.
- Jointly construct proof-reading guides and encourage writers to review their own writing using the checklist.
- Invite writers to set personal goals and monitor their own progress.
- Provide sufficient time for students to reflect on the processes and products of writing so that they can consolidate and extend learning.
- Teach note-taking strategies.
- Show students how to select and synthesise relevant information from a range of different curriculum areas, e.g. use flow charts, retrieval charts, semantic grids and structured overviews.
- Encourage students to jointly construct and use writing frameworks to assist writing organisation.

Teaching Emphases

In this phase:
- help writers to use their knowledge of other texts as models for their own writing
- encourage children to brainstorm, share ideas and talk about their writing to activate their background knowledge before they start to write
- to help ascertain which details should be included in their written text, encourage children to think of the needs of their intended audience by imagining that they are in that role or asking others to assume the audience role.

Writing across Curriculum Areas

Purpose	Maths	Science	Social Studies	Health	Literature	Art/Crafts
Inform or advise			Note on pioneer parade *Parents*			List of art requirements *Teacher*
Direct or instruct	Rules for money game *Peers*	Procedure to set up ant farm *Peers*				
Persuade				Anti-smoking slogan *Unknown*		Poster for Pioneer Day *Peers*
Describe		Movement of ants in ant farm *Self or teacher*				
Compare	Graph results *Self*		Exposition Modern farmers have an easy life *Peers*			
Entertain					Parody of well-known poem or song *Peers*	
Socialise			Letter to penfriend		Rules for use of equipment *Peers*	
Express feelings					Journal response to shared reading *Self*	
Inquire			Letter for info. on pioneer museum *Unknown*	Questionnaire on attitudes to smoking *Unknown*		
Hypothesise or predict	Estimate *Self*	Experiment outcomes *Self*			Written predictions from titles and pictures *Self*	
Learn		Report on ants *Parents, teachers, peers* Notes on experiment *Self and teacher*	Skeleton outline from pioneer text *Self* Notes from pioneer text *Self*	Explanation of respiratory system *Self and teacher*	Story map *Peers* Written retell of chosen story *Partner*	

* Entries in italic face indicate audience

Teachers may wish to show use of writing across the curriculum. Purpose, audience and form are clearly linked.

For Parents

How can I help my child with writing?

- Praise children's writing efforts and respond to the message. Show that you enjoy and value children's writing.
- Ensure that children have access to a modern dictionary that they can use.
- If children have access to a computer, look out for programs which involve reading, writing or spelling for real purposes, rather than those which simply drill spelling out of context, e.g. solving puzzles, making or completing crosswords, choose your own adventure games.
- When children read independently encourage them to talk about what they are reading. If possible read the books so that you have information to talk about. Ask open questions that allow children to discuss, rather than feel as if they are being interrogated, e.g. What was the book about? Which part was the best?
- Read aloud to children. Ask the librarian or teacher for suggested titles. Novels by contemporary authors can provide great serials.
- Encourage children to read newpapers and discuss interesting articles.
- Help children to write letters requesting information or material for school projects.
- Encourage children to write to community newspapers about topics of local interest or to a larger paper on more general topics about which they feel strongly.
- Develop consumer awareness by encouraging children to write to a manufacturer whose product or packaging is unsatisfactory.

Projects: How can parents help?

Many teachers work with children to set guidelines and project plans for children to follow, so talk with children to see what these entail. If you are unable to ascertain what is expected you may need to seek help from the class teacher.

The following strategies are similar to those used in schools and may provide some guidance so that the children actually do the project (not you!).

- Brainstorm and organise
  This strategy helps children to see how they may order information. Brainstorm all ideas related to the topic. Write each idea on a small piece of paper or card. Write everything that is suggested.
  Move the papers to group ideas that seem related to each other. Draw arrows between words from other categories if they seem relevant. Decide on a sub heading for each group. Glue the papers when you are satisfied with groupings. This will provide a plan for the project.

- Make decisions
  Draw two columns on a page. In the first column write *What I know* and list all that they know about the topic. In the second column, *What I want to know*, list questions that they want answered. Decide where information might come from and jot down resources that could be used.

- Gather information
  Encourage children to read for information to answer questions and jot down key words as they read. They then turn the book over and write information using key words as a guide. (This helps reduce the likelihood of children copying slabs of text.) Gather other supporting material that may be useful, e.g. pictures, maps, diagrams etc.

- Set material out under heading and sub headings and arrange other material. Write information in full for each sub heading and then do introduction and conclusion. Other inclusions may be contents page, index, glossary of terms and a bibliography.

- Children may need help to choose and organise appropriate material for projects. This does not mean that parents have to do the whole project. It may be advisable to talk with the children and the class teacher to make sure.

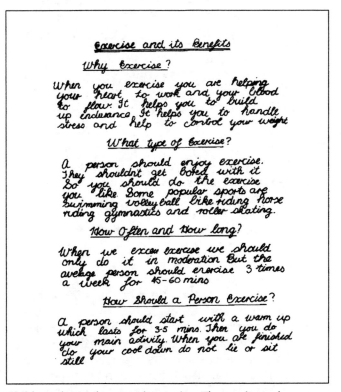

Children don't always write stories. They write to learn, inform, persuade, compare and express feelings. They write for different purposes and audiences.

Proficient Writing

PHASE 5

Writers have developed a personal style of writing and are able to manipulate forms of writing to suit their purposes. They have control over spelling and punctuation. They choose from a wide vocabulary and their writing is cohesive, coherent and satisfying.

Medical treatment was not readily available to the settlers on their isolated homesteads. Mukinbudin was thirty miles from their camp and was visited only once a week by a doctor. In emergencies, the Fitzsimmon family had to travel all the way to Kunonoppin. Mrs Priest can remember mothers using a needle and thread to sew up cuts and gashes. Many people died in the bush because of the hardships and deprivations, these included Mrs Priest's sister and nephew.

Mrs Priest has some sad memories of her time on contract clearing, especially the hard life and the death of her sister and nephew. She can also remember some good things, the beauty of the natural bush and learning to 'make do' with what one had.

Above all, Mrs Priest remembers the friendship of those living in the bush, and, sharing the good and bad times together.

By Jeromy Evans

From this sample we can assume that Jeromy:

◆ **selects text forms to suit purpose and audience, demonstrating control over most essential elements.**
• demonstrates ability to view writing from reader's perspective
• writes a complete, succinct orientation and develops relevant ideas and events
◆ **uses a variety of simple, compound and complex sentences appropriate to text form**
◆ **uses a wide range of words that clearly and precisely convey meaning in a particular form**
• discusses selection of words, clauses or phrases for their shades of meaning and impact on style
◆ **edits own writing during and after composing**

◆ **demonstrates accurate use of punctuation**
• discusses and uses a range of connectors
◆ **writes to define, clarify and develop ideas and express creativity**
◆ **writes a topic sentence and includes relevant information to develop a cohesive paragraph**
◆ **organises paragraphs logically to form a cohesive text**

Proficient Writing Indicators

(See also Phase 4: Transitional Spelling and Stage 5: Independent Spelling of *Spelling: Developmental Continuum*)

Content, Organisation and Contextual Understandings

(See p. 103)

The writer:

◆ **selects text forms to suit purpose and audience, demonstrating control over most essential elements**
◆ **can explain the goals in writing a text and indicate the extent to which they were achieved**
◆ **writes to define, clarify and develop ideas and express creativity, e.g. stories, poems, reports, arguments**
◆ **writes a topic sentence and includes relevant information to develop a cohesive paragraph**
◆ **organises paragraphs logically to form a cohesive text**
◆ **uses a variety of simple, compound and complex sentences appropriate to text form**
• identifies likely audiences and adjusts writing to achieve impact
• conveys a sense of personal involvement in imaginative writing
• conducts research effectively in order to select appropriate information to fulfil task demands
• demonstrates success in writing a wide range of forms, e.g. stories, reports, expository texts, poems, plays
• has sufficient quality ideas to fulfil task demands
• develops topic fully
• uses a plan to organise ideas
• sustains coherence and cohesion throughout text
• demonstrates ability to view writing from a reader's perspective
• expresses a well-reasoned point of view in writing
• can justify a decision in writing
• can write about the same topic from different points of view
• writes a complete, succinct orientation and develops relevant ideas and events
• uses complex sentences with embedded clauses or phrases, e.g. 'My friend Jane, who lives next door, ...'
• discusses and uses a range of linking words, e.g. thus, furthermore, in addition
• signals cause and effect using *if, then, because, so, since, result in, brings about, hence, consequently, subsequently*
• signals comparisons using *like, different from, however, resembles, whereas, similar*
• signals alternatives using *on the other hand, otherwise, conversely, either, instead (of), whether*
• signals time order using *later, meanwhile, subsequently, initially, finally.*

Word Usage

(See p. 105)

The writer:

◆ **uses a wide range of words that clearly and precisely convey meaning in a particular form**
• discusses selection of words, clauses or phrases for their shades of meaning and impact on style
• chooses appropriate words to create atmosphere and mood
• elaborates ideas to convey coherent meaning
• sustains appropriate language throughout, e.g. formal language in a business letter
• uses humour, sarcasm or irony
• uses idioms and colloquialisms to enhance writing
• attempts to involve the reader by the use of metaphor, simile, imagery and other literary devices that require commitment from the reader.

Editing

(See p. 106)

The writer:

◆ **edits own writing during and after composing**
• attempts to re-order words, phrases, clauses and paragraphs to clarify and achieve precise meaning
• uses a revising and editing checklist to improve own writing.

Language Conventions

(See p. 107)

The writer:

◆ **demonstrates accurate use of punctuation**
• demonstrates accurate use of:
  capital letters
  full stops
  commas for a variety of purposes
  quotation marks
  exclamation marks
  apostrophes for contractions
  apostrophes for ownership
  paragraphing
  brackets and dashes
• uses punctuation to enhance meaning.

Strategies

The writer:

- ◆ **takes notes, selects and synthesises relevant information and plans text sequence**
- • evaluates writing of others.

Attitude

The writer:

- • writes for enjoyment, to get things done and for personal expression
- • shows interest in the craft of writing
- • is resourceful in gathering information.

> Many of the people who want to save the tree talk of history and heritage. The tree was a meeting place, a place of happiness, a source of shade on burning summer days after a refreshing swim in the nearby river. But then the traffic built up. The river became a murky passage of sludge. The children grew up and had their own children, but their children knew nothing of this once peaceful place.
>
> Draft

Spelling Indicators

The Key Indicators from the First Steps *Spelling: Developmental Continuum* have been included because learning to spell is part of learning to communicate in written language. For further information about children's spelling development, see the First Steps *Spelling: Developmental Continuum*.

Transitional Spelling Phase
(from sounds to structures)

In this phase, children are moving away from a heavy reliance on the phonetic strategy towards the use of visual and meaning-based strategies. They may still have difficulty recognising if a word 'looks right' but should be able to proof their known bank of words. Writing will show evidence of an increasing bank of known words.

Key Indicators
The writer:
- **uses letters to represent all vowel and consonant sounds in a word, placing vowels in every syllable, e.g. holaday (holiday), gramous (grandma's), castel (castle), relyd (relied), gorrilas (gorillas)**
- **is beginning to use visual strategies such as knowledge of common letter patterns and critical features of words, e.g. silent letters, double letters**

Independent Spelling Phase

In this phase, children have become aware of the many patterns and rules that are characteristic of our spelling system. When spelling a new word they use a multi-strategy approach. They have the ability to recognise when a word doesn't look right and to think of alternative spellings. Spellers in this phase will have accumulated a large bank of known words that they can recall automatically.

Key Indicators
The writer:
- **is aware of the many patterns and rules that are characteristic of the English spelling system, e.g. common English letter patterns, relationship between meaning and spelling**
- **makes generalisations and is able to apply them to new situations, e.g. rules for adding suffixes, selection of appropriate letter patterns (-ion)**
- **accurately spells prefixes, suffixes, contractions, compound words**
- **uses context to distinguish homonyms and homophones**
- **uses silent letters and double consonants correctly**
- **effectively spells words with uncommon spelling patterns and words with irregular spelling, e.g. aisle, quay, liaise**
- **uses less common letter patterns correctly, e.g. weird, forfeit, cough, reign**
- **uses a multi-strategy approach to spelling (visual patterns, sound patterns, meaning)**
- **is able to recognise if a word doesn't look right and to think of alternative spellings**
- **analyses and checks work, editing writing and correcting spelling**
- **recognises word origins and uses this information to make meaningful associations between words**
- **continues to experiment when writing new words**
- **uses spelling references such as dictionaries, thesauruses and resource books appropriately**
- **uses syllabification when spelling new words**
- **has accumulated a large bank of known sight words and is using more sophisticated language**
- **shows increased interest in the similarities, differences, relationships and origins of words**
- **is willing to take risks and responsibilities and is aware of a writer's obligations to readers in the area of spelling**
- **has a positive attitude towards self as a speller**
- **has an interest in words and enjoys using them**
- **is willing to use a range of resources and extend knowledge of words, including derivation, evolution and application**

Strategies Used by Writers

In this phase, writers demonstrate control over all elements of writing. They have been exposed to a variety of forms of text in both reading and writing, and they understand that purpose and audience dictate the form. They see writing as a skill to be used across the curriculum.

Environmental Print

Writers consult many written texts to assist the development of writing. They also consciously choose written language structures that support and enhance meaning.

Interaction

Authors continually evaluate and reflect upon their own and other's writing. They analyse many forms of writing and make judgments based on their knowledge of particular forms, purposes and audiences. They try to read their writing from the perspective of another reader.

Editing

Writers manipulate forms of writing to suit their purposes. They have control over spelling and punctuation, and are able to choose from a wide vocabulary. Their writing is cohesive, coherent and satisfying. They try to read their writing from another's perspective and make appropriate changes.

Reflection

Writers reflect on their writing and reading. They make generalisations and apply their knowledge to assist them in new contexts.

PASSIVE EMOTIONS

A story to promote non-smoking

The small lounge-room was completely dark except for a thin strip of dismal, grey light which shone through a gap between the curtains from a street lamp outside. The room was shrouded in smoke, cigarette smoke. It was thickest in the darkest corner of the room. In this corner, sitting in a rocking chair, was a balding, middle-aged man.

The few thin strands on his hair lifted in the slight breeze created by a fan standing across the room. His clothes reeked of the foul smelling smoke. His wrinkled face looked as if he was mourning something, or someone, he had cherished. From one of his hands came the dull red glow of a cigarette. He seemed oblivious to the world around him. Lost deep in his mind and memories of a happier past.

A tear trickled simply down his cheek while his eyes were locked on a photograph he was holding in his hand. From the picture a beautiful young bride in a floral dress smiled up at him. She had been his wife and he had loved her like life itself. Two days ago she had died prematurely, and painfully from lung cancer.

'Smoking related' the doctor had said. Yet she had never once smoked in all her life. She had been a passive smoker.

He remembered how they used to sit together, arms around each other. As he enjoyed his cigarettes she would inhale the smoke he expelled. Throughout their twenty years of happy marriage she had continually, gently lovingly urged him to stop smoking, but all in vain. He had shunned the idea, never listening to her. She had always said smoking was endangering his life. Neither of them had imagined her life was under threat. Now she was gone from him forever.

He looked down at the cigarette in his hand and watched the white paper blackening and disappear in smoke. The tiny red glow slowly burning its way towards his fingers, releasing the poisons which had killed her and were probably killing him. He felt the rage and grief well up inside him and focus on the tiny tube of tobacco. Then suddenly, with a violent jab of his hand, he crushed the murderous thing, extinguishing the burning tip, and cursed the day he had first set one of those deadly cigarettes to his lips.

Tim

Teaching Notes

A varied program that enables students to write a range of forms of texts and to analyse and reflect upon different types of literature will assist writers in this phase. Text types typically include essays, novels, personal and business letters, job applications, play, film and television scripts, newspaper articles, literary criticisms and analysis of mass media.

This document does not include specific advanced activities for students in this phase. Teachers in different subject disciplines should take responsibility for teaching the type of writing they require from students.

Major Teaching Emphases

- ◆ **provide opportunities for students to analyse, evaluate and structure an extensive variety of forms of text, both narrative and informational**
- ◆ **discuss the specific effect of context, audience and purpose on written texts**
- ◆ **extend students' knowledge of correct use of writing conventions**
- ◆ **teach students to analyse mass media**
- ◆ **discuss and foster a sense of 'personal voice', e.g. individual style, tone, rhythm, vocabulary**
- ◆ **extend the students' range of planning and revision strategies**
- ◆ **encourage students to use writing to reflect on and monitor their own learning**
- ◆ **encourage students to read as writers and write as readers**
- • provide opportunities for students to write and manipulate forms of text for a variety of purposes and audiences
- • encourage students to reflect on their own writing
- • encourage students to analyse their writing critically
- • encourage students to read widely and reflect on what is read
- • encourage students to discuss authors' writing styles and the ways in which authors position or manipulate readers
- • increase students' exposure to language that enables them to talk about language
- • continue reading aloud to enable students to appreciate patterns, rhythms and nuances of language
- • provide opportunities to develop, refine and use new vocabulary

At all phases:
- ◆ **model good English language use**
- ◆ **model writing every day**
- ◆ **encourage students to reflect on their understandings, gradually building a complete picture of written language structures**
- ◆ **ensure that students have opportunities to write for a variety of audiences and purposes**
- ◆ **encourage students to share their writing experiences.**

◆ *Entries in bold are considered critical to the children's further development*

Establishing an Environment for Language Learning

In this phase of development, students are independent writers. They require, however, some guidance as they approach more complex and demanding writing tasks. The environment should enable full discussion and debate about a variety of written texts and students should be challenged to justify, generalise, compare, refer to and evaluate their reading, both orally and in writing. They should also be given adequate opportunity to extrapolate and apply information in all subject areas and translate that information into writing that will satisfy the demands of the particular subject area.

Ways to Create an Environment for Language Learning

- Provide a supportive environment that enables students to feel able to express opinions that may differ from those of the teacher.
- Continue to foster independence and self-reliance.
- Allow time for journal writing or other personal writing.
- Provide opportunities for students to write to learn, inform, persuade, express feelings, communicate and entertain.
- Set clear purposes and audiences for writing across all curriculum areas.
- Use questioning to guide students in making decisions about which text forms to use.
- Encourage students to be aware of factors that affect the way meaning is constructed, e.g. culture, linguistic knowledge, topic knowledge etc.
- Plan activities that require students to work independently.
- Encourage students to take responsibility for their own writing development.
- Encourage students to aim for conventional spelling of a wide variety of words.

Grouping Arrangements

Flexibility is the essential ingredient when considering group arrangements. The type, size and composition of groups is determined by the needs of class members and by the purpose for forming the group. Individual, pairs, small-group and class-group arrangements are all necessary at different times for writing. For example, you might form a small group to teach punctuation skills, take the class through a session on writing headlines and work with an individual on sequencing, all within a few days.

(a) Individual writing forms a major portion of writing time because the emphasis is on individual development. Individuals:
- make decisions about their writing
- draft
- perform initial revising and editing.

(b) Writers may work with another person — classmate or you — to:
- share ideas
- revise and edit
- ask opinions and questions
- seek support and guidance.

(c) Small groups can be useful for:
- teaching students with common needs
- compiling group writing
- sharing work and seeking response
- planning and making decisions.

(d) Class sessions can be organised for:
- sharing literature
- sharing and responding to writing
- teaching a new skill
- compiling a class piece of writing
- modelling a process or product.

Endeavour to use all types of grouping arrangements because each one provides a particular learning experience that offers something different to writers.

Encourage students to take responsibility for their writing development by:
- setting and monitoring personal goals
- using a reflective journal to evaluate their reading and writing
- keeping a reading and writing log to build a list of achievements
- keeping a list of forms and purposes for writing
- keeping a record of conferences.

Content, Organisation and Contextual Understandings

(See p. 97)

Students in this phase demonstrate control over the conventions of a wide range of forms of text and make selections appropriate to the task. They choose an organisational framework relevant to the purpose of the task and their ideas are clearly ordered within that framework. They use organisational markers appropriate to the form of text (e.g. titles, headings, layout, paragraphs). Each paragraph or section is focused on one idea and relates logically to the next to form a cohesive and coherent whole.

First Steps *Writing: Resource Book* provides strategies and suggestions for introducing a range of written forms and information to help teachers assess students' progress in writing some forms of text.

- **Introduction of More Complex Forms of Writing**
  Establish the purpose and audience for writing before introducing a new form. Gather several examples of quality writing in the form to be taught and share with the students. Discuss why these pieces are successful. Record some of the common features found in the writing. Discuss and chart these to leave on display for writers to use. Demonstrate the form on the overhead projector and talk about the writing process. Encourage writers to participate in the process. Provide time for students to practise writing the form and to share their efforts. Interact with students in a positive way. Discuss aspects of the writing with students, e.g. its intended purpose, suitability for audience etc.

- **Retelling**
  Before writers attempt a retell, the teacher should present several examples of the particular text type to be used, e.g. reports, myths or fables. Students discuss features of the form. For the retell, each student requires a copy of the text. Students read the title and write predictions about the plot. They also list words or phrases likely to be encountered. Predictions are shared with the class. Teacher reads text aloud and then children read it silently. Students write their retell for someone who has not read the text. They do not refer to the text. Students then compare, clarify and justify their retell with a partner.

- **Follow the Lead**
  Work in groups. Teacher writes a topic sentence. The first group member writes a sentence and passes it on to the next member, who writes an appropriate sentence. He or she folds the sheet so that only this sentence is seen, and passes it on. After all members have written a sentence, the whole group reads the

text and attempts an ending. Discuss the text with the class. Focus on the way one sentence follows on from the previous sentence and the relationship between the sentences.

- **Another Slant**
  Select a well known traditional story and read it to students. Discuss the author's point of view (these stories are usually written from the narrator's stance). Students then write the same story from the point of view of one of the characters in the story. Discuss how this changes the style and perception of the story.

- **What's My Style?**
  Students each select a short paragraph from a book. They write one sentence of their own into the paragraph without showing others. Working in groups, each student reads the selected paragraph, including own sentence. Group members try to identify which sentence has been inserted and discuss why they chose that sentence.

- **Advertisement Analysis**
  Students examine advertisements in different types of magazines. Discuss why they are different (audience interest). Teacher selects an advertisement and models how it might be modified if it were to appear in a publication that has a different audience, e.g. political journals, teenage magazines, fashion catalogues.

- **Time Warp**
  Discuss changes that might occur if a particular story was written in a different era. Students attempt to write a modern version of a well-known tale, e.g. *Snow White*. Share the products and discuss the processes needed to achieve the purpose.

- **Add Your Reason**
  Students work with a partner. Each writes a sentence. The sentence should express a reason supporting a point, e.g. Students should have tasks to do at home because it makes them responsible. Partners then write

two other reasons supporting the same argument. Discuss, highlight similarities and differences and compare to original sentences.

- **At the End**
Teacher asks students for three words. The words are written on the board. The class then makes up sentences that end in one of those words. Sentences such as *How do you spell __?* or *He said __* are excluded because a word can always be used in this way. Words such as *a, an,* and *the* are excluded. Divide group into two teams. Team 1 assigns Team 2 a word. Team 2 writes a sentence (on the board) that ends in that word. The object is to stump the opposition team. Any word that can not be dealt with during the game is noted and referred to at a later time to see if it can be used at the end of the sentence.

- **Journal**
Encourage students to keep a response book while they are reading novels or other material. Students write what they were thinking about, questions which arise, or their feelings after stopping at a logical point. (This could replace a book report.)

- Continue to use opportunities across the curriculum to encourage students to develop persuasive writing skills.

- Choose a specific relevant issue, e.g. 'Homework should be abolished', and ask students to take a stand and to justify or support the stance taken. Small-group discussion should precede written work. Students need to understand that justifications must be based on fact and that deliberate distortion is unacceptable in this context. Arguments must be presented in logical order and emotive language may be used to influence the reader.

- Collect a range of weekend newspapers. Select one news item and compare the relevant article from each paper. Discuss any similarities or differences. In groups, students discuss how they could report the news item from a different perspective or point of view. Students then write their versions of the item. Further discussion should focus on the strategies used by students to complete the task.

- **Letters to the Editor**
From newspapers, collect letters to the editor over a period of a week. Classify them into broad categories, e.g. letters about conservation issues, political issues, or education issues. In groups, students analyse one set of letters. Discuss features such as point of view, use of emotive language and structure of the text. Students then choose an issue and write their own letters to the editor.

Word Usage

(see p. 97)

Students in this phase use a wide variety of words that clearly convey meaning. Many of these words are precise and reflect shades of meaning as well as an understanding of their impact on style.

These activities can help children develop their word awareness and extend their vocabulary.

- Be Precise
  Students work in pairs. The student draws a simple picture and then writes instructions so that a partner can reproduce the picture accurately using only the written instructions as a guide. When each picture is completed, it is returned to the owner who compares it with the original and modifies the written directions. Students then move to a new partner and the process is repeated. Success is achieved when the picture produced closely resembles the original.

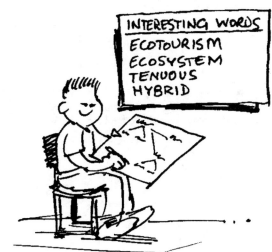

- Guess the Words
  Each student is given a card with a noun written on it. Concrete nouns may be more suitable for younger writers, while abstract nouns may be more appropriate for older students. Students write a definition of their noun without mentioning the word. Class tries to guess what the noun is. If there is more than one answer that fits, the writer must refine the definition unless it can genuinely apply to two words. Two teams compete and each team tries to find as many alternative words that fit the definitions offered by the opposing team. The team with the most alternatives wins.

- Group Discussion
  First Steps *Oral Language: Resource Book* offers many suggestions for developing descriptive and objective language. The activities link directly to writing.

Editing

(See p. 97)

Students independently revise during and after composing. Where appropriate, this includes restructuring of words, phrases, clauses and paragraphs to clarify meaning and enhance coherence. They also proof read to correct spelling, punctuation and grammar.

Word processing programs provide ideal structures to assist the editing process.

When revising and editing their writing, students need to understand that the emphasis should be on clarifying the meaning of the text. They need to consider the intended audience, the purpose and the form of writing.

Audience

When considering the audience, students might ask the following questions:
- Is the language formal enough?
- Has enough detail been provided?
- Will the audience understand the words used?
- Will the writing achieve the desired effect on the audience?

Purpose

When considering the purpose of writing, students might ask the following questions:
- What was the purpose? e.g. to inform, persuade, entertain, describe etc.
- Does the writing achieve the designated purpose?
- Can change be made to achieve the purpose?

Form

The form chosen is dictated by the purpose and audience. When considering the form, students might ask the following questions:
- Is the form appropriate for the audience and purpose?
- Are the conventions of the form evident?
- See also editing suggestions in the *Conventional Writing Phase* (p. 90).
- Make use of word processing programs to assist writing and editing skills.

Language Conventions
(See p. 97)

Students use correct terminology when they discuss various parts of speech. Their written language indicates that they understand how the English language is structured.

Punctuation and Grammar

Students understand that punctuation conventions vary according to the form of text and that conventions may be broken to achieve stylistic impact.

Punctuation and grammar conventions should always be taught in context. Situations that provide contexts for this are:

- modelled writing sessions
- when students are editing their work
- when students are participating in text innovation
- when reading.

Writers should demonstrate they can:

- maintain subject-verb, noun-pronoun agreement
- construct, and correctly use, phrases and subordinate clauses
- use prepositions, adjectives and adverbs correctly
- maintain consistency of tense and point of view
- use capital letters and full stops
- use commas for items in a series, to separate words, names and speech in a sentence, and to separate embedded phrases and clauses
- use quotation marks, question marks, exclamation marks, apostrophes and paragraphing correctly
- achieve some success when using dashes, brackets, semicolons and colons
- demonstrate overall legibility and neatness when presenting writing
- use a layout appropriate to the writing form, e.g. headings for reports or speech bubbles in a cartoon
- use graphics to clarify written text, where appropriate
- use complex logical structures to provide authenticity
- express actions as things (nominalisation) to make arguments seem more objective
- use a variety of verbs, often in passive voice, e.g. 'It is believed ...'
- conceal personal bias by use of objective language.

Spelling

For activities and strategies to use in spelling, consult the First Steps *Spelling: Development Continuum*.
Encourage students to:

- spell words from a wide vocabulary
- make close approximations, based on knowledge of English spelling patterns, whenever non-conventional spelling is used, e.g. 'maintainance' for 'maintenance'
- consult a thesaurus or dictionary
- extend their knowledge of the spelling system.

For Parents

How can I help my child with writing?

- Provide a quiet study area for children.
- Be prepared to discuss writing tasks with children.
- Encourage children to continue to read and write for information and pleasure.
- Take children to see suitable 'live' theatre performances.
- Discuss current events.
- Talk about the mass media and their influence on society.
- Encourage children to use writing to get things done, e.g. letters to politicians, newspapers etc.
- Encourage children to use writing to express their feelings. Respect their privacy if they choose to keep personal diaries or letters.
- Play word games, talk about word meanings.
- Encourage children to use dictionaries and thesauruses independently.
- Understand that the process of writing and refining writing for publication takes time.
- Understand that writing is for different purposes and audiences.
- Understand that different types of writing require different language, setting out and special vocabulary, e.g. a business letter is not the same as a letter to a pen pal.

Name of Insect	How Useful to Man.
1 Bee - Hymenoptera	Bees are useful as they pollinate plants to cause the growing of the fruit.
2 Ladybug - Coleoptera.	These help by eating insects such as aphids.
3 Bee - Hymenoptera	these provide man with enterprises such as honey and beeswax.
4 Silk Moth - Lepidoptera.	These provide man with his silk enterprise.
5 Cochineal Bug - Coleoptera.	These insects when dead and dry are used to make natural dyes - scarlet, carmine and crimson.
6 Cockroaches - Coleoptera	Cockroaches are scavengers and clean-up crumbs and scraps of food.
7 Dung Beetles - Coleoptera	These feed on manure and it's used for putting nutrients in soil.
8 Wasp - Hymenoptera.	Pollinate flowers.
9 Ant - Hymenoptera	These eat plants and insects. Ants Also are an important food source for birds, lizards etc. They are also sold chocolate-coated as a delicacy.
10 Termites - Isoptera.	These are roasted and eaten by the handful in Africa.

When the purpose of writing changes, so does the form.

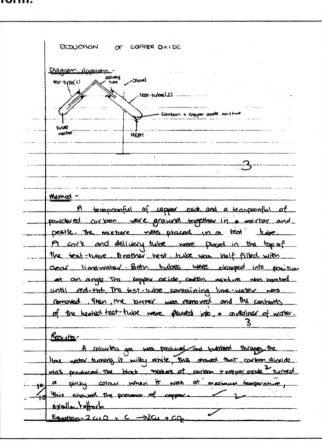

The Agricultural Revolution 1760-1830

The agricultural revolution was a slow process of change. During this revolution there was a system known as "the openfield system". This system meant that all fields were open, cattle could wander over them and eat yields. Each paddock was divided into strips so landowners would have a fair amount of good or bad land. This also enabled the farmers to produce corn and wheat for beer and bread for the rising population.

Most of the pre-agrarian rev. was of the subsistence type. This meant that the farmers would produce enough food for his family plus some surplus to buy other necessities.

Soon people realised this was an impractical way of farming because of the growing population which needed a much larger amount of food. Soon a method of enclosing the farms was introduced. They began to enclose the common and waste lands to prevent cattle entering fields. This soon became an essential part of farming so if poor farmer could not afford to enclose their property they were forced to sell to larger landowners. Soon all the farmers who could not afford to keep their own land soon became jobless and moved to the city to find work.

REDUCTION OF COPPER OXIDE

Diagram. Apparatus -
test-type (2)   delivery tube   stand
Test-tube (1)
Carbon + copper oxide mixture
lime water
HEAT

3

Method -
A teaspoonful of copper oxide and a teaspoonful of powdered carbon were ground together in a mortar and pestle. The mixture was placed in a test tube. A cork and delivery tube were placed in the top of the test-tube. Another test-tube was half filled with clear lime-water. Both tubes were clamped into position at an angle. The copper oxide, carbon mixture was heated until red-hot. The test-tube containing lime-water was removed. Then, the burner was removed and the contents of the heated test-tube were poured into a container of water.

3

Results:
A colourless gas was produced and bubbled through the lime water turning it milky white. This showed that carbon dioxide was produced. The black mixture of carbon + copper oxide turned a pinky colour when it was at maximum temperature, this showed the presence of copper.
excellent effort
Equation - 2CuO + C → 2Cu + CO₂

PHASE **6** Advanced Writing Indicators

(See also Phase 5: Independent Spelling of *Spelling: Developmental Continuum*)

Content, Organisation and Contextual Understandings

The writer:

- controls effectively the language and structural features of a large repertoire of text forms
- controls and manipulates the linguistic and structural components of writing to enhance clarity and impact
- generates, explores and develops topics and ideas
- may choose to manipulate or abandon conventional text forms to achieve impact
- maintains stylistic features throughout texts
- makes critical choices of tone and point of view to suit different purposes and to influence audiences
- writes exploring and developing abstract ideas
- makes informed choices about the linguistic features, organisation and development of ideas and information according to audience and purpose
- deliberately structures sentences to enhance a text and according to audience and purpose
- develops ideas and information clearly, sustaining coherence throughout complex texts
- conceals personal bias where appropriate.

Word Usage

The writer:

- selects and manipulates words, phrases or clauses, for their shades of meaning and impact
- successfully involves the reader by the use of literary devices such as metaphor, simile, onomatopoeia
- uses abstract and technical terms appropriately in context.

Editing

The writer:

- modifies and restructures phrases, clauses, paragraphs or whole texts to clarify and achieve precise meaning.

Language Conventions

The writer:

- controls the conventions of writing but may make a deliberate choice to break them to enhance meaning.

Strategies

The writer:

- takes responsibility for planning, revising and proof reading to ensure that writing achieves its purpose
- reflects on, and critically evaluates own writing to ensure that content and organisation suit the purpose for writing and the audience
- evaluates and synthesises information from a variety of sources to support view.

Attitude

The writer:

- responds to a compulsion to write
- reflects on, critically evaluates and critiques own writing and that of others.

Part IV

Profiles of Writing Development

To make recording easier for teachers, student profile sheets, that can be photocopied, are included in this book. They enable teachers to record the progress of individual students, and to compile a class profile.

The following records are included:

- student's profile sheets for self-assessment
- whole class profile sheets using all the indicators
- whole class profile sheets using key indicators only.

Note:
An individual student profile sheet that will record progress throughout the primary years is included as a fold-out at the beginning of this book.

Student's Profile Sheets

The student's profile sheets for each phase provide lists of skills, understandings, strategies and attitudes that both the student and teacher can look for when assessing writing development.

Why use Student's Profile Sheets?

Students and teachers can work together to set and monitor goals in writing, using the profile sheets. Students could also be encouraged to show their parents when entries are made on the sheet.

How to use the Student's Profile Sheets

The profile sheets can be kept in student's writing files and updated from time to time, perhaps in student/teacher conferences. Young students may need help to use the sheets but older students can be encouraged to take responsibility for their own writing development.

When would you use the Student's Profile Sheets?

The student's profile sheets can be used at regular intervals or incidentally during writing conferences.

PHASE 1: Role Play Writing

Name:_____ Date:_____

Look what I can do	not yet	some-times	always
• Have-a-go at writing on my own.			
• Try to write some letters of the alphabet.			
• Try to write my own name.			
• Write 'messages' or 'lists'.			
• 'Read' my own 'writing'.			
• Point to where writing starts.			
• Point to pictures.			
• Point to words when I read.			
• Talk about things I am writing.			
• Talk about some signs I see in shops or in the street.			
I like: • 'writing' just for fun			
• showing people what I can write			
• listening to stories			
• joining in with stories as they are told			
• listening to my favourite stories and rhymes.			

Here are some letters of the alphabet I can write:

PHASE 2: Experimental Writing

Name:_____Date:_____

Look what I can do	not yet	some-times	always
• Have-a-go at writing on my own.			
• Tell others what I have written.			
• Try to write lists, stories, messages, signs, cards and letters.			
• Write about things I can do.			
• Write some letters from the alphabet.			
• Say the alphabet and point to each letter.			
• Sound-out some words as I write them.			
• Write some words correctly.			
• Point to each word as I say it.			
• Copy some words I need.			
• Leave a space between each word.			
I like: • writing for myself and other people			
• telling people about my writing			
• seeing my writing pinned up for everyone to read			
• showing other people what I have written			
• reading stories and having them read to me			
• reading stories			
• telling about things I have done and places I have been.			

PHASE 3: Early Writing

Name:_____ Date:_____

Look what I can do	not yet	some-times	always
• Choose interesting things to write about.			
• Explain why I am writing.			
• Write recounts, procedures, stories, letters, lists, labels, signs and other interesting things that I need to write.			
• Find some parts of my writing that need to be improved.			
• Mark some words in my writing that I am not sure of.			
• Talk about my plans for writing.			
• Re-read my writing to make sure it makes sense.			
• Use our class checklist to help me edit my work.			
• Share my ideas for writing.			
• Listen to other people's writing and make suggestions to improve it.			
• Sound-out words.			
• Use word banks and class charts to help me with my spelling when I write.			
I like: • writing for fun			
• being able to finish my writing			
• to see others enjoy my stories			
• showing others what I write			
• talking about what I am going to write.			

PHASE 4: Conventional Writing

Name:_____Date:_____

Look what I can do	not yet	some-times	always
• Write for different purposes and audiences, e.g. a story for the class library, an advertisement for the school fete, a set of instructions for a game, a report on Australian animals, a letter to invite a guest speaker to visit.			
• See the difference between books that are written to give factual information and books that tell a story.			
• Plan my writing so that I develop the main idea and include supporting material that adds information and interest.			
• Brainstorm to see what I already know about a topic.			
• Make notes and gather information from things that I read.			
• Classify the information I have and decide whether I need to find more information in a particular area before I start writing.			
• Organise my writing using headings and sub headings.			
• Write a main sentence and add relevant information to develop a paragraph.			
• Make sure that one paragraph logically leads to the next.			
• Choose a story title that will make the reader want to read-on.			
• Include all the necessary details to set the scene of a story.			
• Include dialogue to develop the plot of a story or to give the reader more information about a character.			
• Develop characters that are believable by including interesting details about their personalities, actions and reactions.			

PHASE 4: Conventional Writing (continued)

Look what I can do	not yet	some-times	always
• Build up excitement in a story by including interesting details.			
• Use repetition for emphasis, e.g. 'Let's all be very, very quiet,' she whispered.			
• Talk about ways that published authors 'hook' readers and keep them interested.			
• Use adverbs and adjectives to elaborate for the reader.			

• Use the following punctuation:
  – capital letters for proper nouns, titles and to start sentences
  – question marks
  – exclamation marks
  – apostrophes and contractions
  – apostrophes for possession
  – quotation marks for dialogue
  – brackets to include additional information.			

• Combine short sentences to form a more interesting sentence.			
• Proof read and revise my own writing using our editing checklist.			
• Cut and paste text to reorder the ideas and clarify meaning.			
• Use a dictionary to check my spelling.			
• Choose better words for commonly overused ones like 'said' or 'nice'.			
• Set personal goals to improve my writing.			
• Keep records of what I have written using a writing log, e.g. Title Date Form and Purpose Audience			

PHASE 5: Proficient Writing

Name:_____Date:_____

Look what I can do	not yet	some-times	always
• Select text forms to suit different purposes and audiences.			
• Read as a writer.			
• Plan before I write.			
• Explain why I make decisions about what to include in my writing.			
• Write from different points of view.			
• Brainstorm to see what I already know about a topic.			
• Make notes and gather information from things that I read then classify the information appropriately.			
• Organise writing using headings and sub headings where appropriate.			
• Make sure that one paragraph leads logically to the next.			
• Write a main sentence and add relevant information to develop a paragraph.			
• Include all the necessary details to set the scene of a story.			
• Include dialogue to develop the plot of a story or to give the reader more information about a character.			
• Develop characters that are believable by including interesting details about their personalities, actions and reactions.			

PHASE 5: Proficient Writing (continued)

Look what I can do	not yet	some-times	always
• Build up excitement and suspense in a story by including intriguing details.			
• Use different ways to 'hook' readers and keep them interested in reading-on.			
• Use technical vocabulary appropriate to particular subjects and topics.			
• Use a wide range of precise vocabulary to elaborate for the reader.			
• Select particular words or phrases for their shades of meaning.			
• Use correct punctuation, e.g. – capital letters for proper nouns, titles and to start sentences – question marks – exclamation marks – apostrophes and contractions – apostrophes for possession – quotation marks for dialogue – brackets to include additional information.			
• Use a dictionary or a spell check program to check my spelling.			
• Cut and paste text to reorder and clarify meaning.			
• Proof read and revise my own writing.			
• Critically evaluate writing of others to identify point of view or position taken.			
• Set and review personal goals to improve my writing.			

Whole Class Profile Sheets

The class profile sheets have all indicators from the Writing Developmental Continuum presented phase by phase so that teachers can enter information about children's progress in writing. The sheets can be photocopied as required.

Why use Class Profile Sheets?

The class profile sheets enable teachers to develop a comprehensive class profile on which to base planning and programming decisions.

How to use the Class Profile Sheets?

- Collect samples of writing
- Observe children's writing behaviours
- Highlight indicators observed
- Write entry date and highlighter colour used

When would you use Class Profile Sheets?

Although teachers make ongoing observations of children's progress, they may formally update information on the continuum two or three times each year (perhaps before report times).

CLASS _____

ROLE PLAY WRITING INDICATORS

Students' Names

The Writer:

Content, Organisation and Contextual Understandings

◆ **assigns a message to own symbols**

◆ **understands that writing and drawing are different, e.g. points to words while 'reading'**

◆ **is aware that print carries a message**

- orally recounts own experiences
- knows some favourite parts of stories, rhymes, jingles or songs
- reads text from memory or invents meaning (the meaning may change each time)
- writes and asks others to assign meaning to what has been written
- talks about own drawing and writing
- tells adults what to write, e.g.' This is my cat'
- role plays writing messages for purpose, e.g. telephone messages
- states purpose for own 'writing', e.g. 'This is my shopping list'
- recognises own name (or part of it) in print, e.g. 'My name starts with that'
- attempts to write own name
- thinks own 'writing' can be read by others

Concepts and Conventions

◆ **uses known letters or approximations of letters to represent written language**

◆ **shows beginning awareness of directionality, i.e. points to where print begins**

- draws symbols consisting of straight, curved or intersecting lines that simulate letters
- makes random marks on paper
- produces aimless or circular scribble
- makes horizontal or linear scribble with some breaks
- places letters randomly on page

continued on next page

Teacher's Notes:

Dates:

CLASS _____

ROLE PLAY WRITING INDICATORS (continued)

Students' Names

The Writer:

Concepts and Conventions (continued)

- writes random strings of letters
- mixes letters, numerals and invented letter shapes
- flips or reverses letters
- makes organisational decisions about writing, e.g. 'I'll start here so it will fit'
- copies layout of some text forms, e.g. letters, lists

Strategies

- experiments with upper and lower case letters. May show a preference for upper case
- repeats a few known alphabet symbols frequently using letters from own name
- copies print from environment

Attitude

- enjoys stories and asks for them to be retold or re-read
- listens attentively to the telling or reading of stories and other texts
- 'writes' spontaneously for self rather than for an audience.

Teacher's Notes:

Dates:

CLASS _____

EXPERIMENTAL WRITING INDICATORS

Students' Names

The Writer:

Content, Organisation and Contextual Understandings

◆ **reads back own writing**

◆ **attempts familiar forms of writing, e.g. lists, letters, recounts, stories, messages**

◆ **writes using simplified oral language structures, e.g. 'I brt loles'**

◆ **uses writing to convey meaning**

• voices thoughts while writing

• writes to communicate messages, direct experiences or feelings

• assumes that reader shares the context so may not give sufficient background information, e.g. may tell 'who' but not 'when'

• often begins sentence with 'I' or 'We'

• is beginning to use written language structures. Has a sense of sentence, i.e. writes complete sentences with or without punctuation

• repeats familiar words when writing, e.g. cat, cat, cat

• generates writing by repeating the same beginning patterns, e.g. 'I like cats, I like dogs, I like birds …'

• recognises some words and letters in context

• recognises that people use writing to convey meaning

Concepts and Conventions

◆ **realises that print contains a constant message**

◆ **uses left to right and top to bottom orientation of print**

◆ **demonstrates one-to-one correspondence between written and spoken words**

• uses upper and lower case letters indiscriminately

• distinguishes between numerals and letters

• leaves a space between word-like clusters of letters

• dictates slowly so teacher can 'keep up' while scribing.

continued on next page

Teacher's Notes:

Dates:

CLASS _____

EXPERIMENTAL WRITING INDICATORS (continued)

Students' Names

The Writer:

Strategies

◆ **relies heavily on the most obvious sounds of a word**

• tells others what has been written

• asks others what has been written

• traces and copies letters with some successful formations

• points to 'words' while reading own writing

• voices thoughts while writing

• reads back what has been written to clarify meaning

• experiments with, and overgeneralises print conventions, e.g. puts a full stop after each word

• uses knowledge of rhyme to spell words written

• uses print resources in classroom, e.g. charts, signs, word banks

Attitude

• listens attentively to the telling or reading of stories and other texts

• writes spontaneously for self or chosen audience.

Teacher's Notes:

Dates:

CLASS

EARLY WRITING INDICATORS

Students' Names

The Writer:

Content, Organisation and Contextual Understandings

◆ **uses a small range of familiar text forms**

◆ **chooses topics that are personally significant**

◆ **uses basic sentence structures and varies sentence beginnings**

◆ **can explain in context, some of the purposes of using writing, e.g. shopping list or telephone messages as a memory aid**

• uses a partial organisational framework, e.g. simple orientation and story development

• often writes a simple recount of personal events or observations and comments

• uses time order to sequence and organise writing

• is beginning to use some narrative structure

• is beginning to use some informational text structures, e.g. recipes, factual description

• writes simple factual accounts with little elaboration

• includes irrelevant detail in 'dawn-to-dark' recounts

• attempts to orient, or create a context for the reader, but may assume a shared context

• rewrites known stories in sequence

• includes detail in written retell

• includes several items of information about a topic

• is beginning to use 'book' language, e.g. 'By the fire sat a cat'.

• joins simple sentences (often overusing the same connectors, e.g. 'and', 'then')

• uses knowledge of rhyme, rhythm and repetition in writing

• repeats familiar patterns, e.g. 'In the jungle I saw ....'

continued on next page
Teacher's Notes:

Dates:

CLASS

EARLY WRITING INDICATORS (continued)

Students' Names

The Writer:

Word Usage

◆ **experiments with words drawn from language experience activites, literature, media and oral language of peers and others**

• discusses word formations and meanings; noticing similarities and differences

• transfers words encountered in talk, or reading, to writing

• highlights words for emphasis, e.g. BIG

Editing

◆ **begins to develop editing skills**

• deletes words to clarify meaning

• adds words to clarify meaning —

• begins to proof read for spelling errors

• responds to requests for clarification

• attempts the use of a proof-reading guide constructed jointly by students and teacher

Language Conventions

◆ **attempts to use some punctuation**

• sometimes uses full stops

• sometimes uses a capital letter to start a sentence

• uses capital letters for names

• attempts use of question marks

• attempts use of exclamation marks

• sometimes uses apostrophes for contractions

• overgeneralises use of print conventions, e.g. overuse of apostrophes, full stops, dashes and commas

• often writes in the first person.

continued on next page

Teacher's Notes:

Dates:

CLASS

EARLY WRITING INDICATORS (continued)

Student's' Names

The Writer:

Language Conventions (continued)

- attempts writing in both first and third person
- usually uses appropriate subject/verb agreements
- usually maintains consistent tense
- writes a title which reflects content

Strategies

- ◆ **talks with others to plan and revise own writing**
- re-reads own writing to maintain word sequence
- attempts to transfer knowledge of text structure to writing, e.g. imitates form of a familiar big book
- shares ideas for writing with peers or teacher
- participates in group brainstorming activities to elicit ideas and information before writing
- in consultation with teacher, sets personal goals for writing development
- discusses proof-reading strategies with peers and teacher and attempts to use them in context

Attitude

- perseveres to complete writing tasks.

Teacher's Notes:

Dates:

CLASS _____

Student's Names

CONVENTIONAL WRITING INDICATORS

The Writer:

Content and Organisation and Contextual Understandings

◆ **uses text forms to suit purpose and audience**

◆ **can explain why some text forms may be more appropriate than others to achieve a specific purpose**

◆ **writes a range of text forms including stories, reports, procedures and expositions**

◆ **uses a variety of simple, compound and extended sentences**

◆ **groups sentences containing related information into paragraphs**

• takes account of some aspects of context, purpose and audience

• considers the needs of audience and includes background information

• uses rhyme, rhythm and repetition for effect (where appropriate)

• demonstrates the ability to develop a topic

• demonstrates knowledge of differences between narrative and informational text when writing

• organises the structure of writing more effectively, e.g. uses headings, sub headings

• can write from another's point of view

• shows evidence of personal voice (where appropriate)

• is developing a personal style of writing

• establishes place, time and situation

• often includes dialogue

• uses dialogue to enhance character development

• shows evidence of the transfer of literary language from reading to writing

• organises paragraphs logically

• uses titles and headings appropriately

• orders ideas in time order or other sequences such as priority order

• uses a variety of linking words such as _and, so, because, if, next, after, before, first._

continued on next page

Teacher's Notes:

Dates:

CLASS _____

CONVENTIONAL WRITING INDICATORS (continued)

Students' Names

The Writer:

Word Usage

◆ **is beginning to select vocabulary according to the demands of audience and purpose, e.g. uses subject-specific vocabulary**

• uses some similes or metaphors in an attempt to enhance meaning

• varies vocabulary for interest

• includes specific vocabulary to explain or describe, e.g. appropriate adjectives

• uses adverbs and adjectives to enhance meaning

• uses simple colloquialisms and clichés

Editing

◆ **uses proof-reading guide or checklist to edit own or peers' writing**

• edits and proof reads own writing after composing

• reorders text to clarify meaning, e.g. moves words, phrases and clauses

• reorders words to clarify meaning

• attempts to correct punctuation

• recognises most misspelled words and attempts corrections

Language Conventions

◆ **punctuates simple sentences correctly**

• uses capital letters for proper nouns

• uses capital letters to start sentences

• uses capital letters for titles

• uses full stops to end sentences

• uses question marks correctly

• sometimes uses commas

• uses apostrophes for possession

continued on next page
Teacher's Notes:

Dates:

CLASS _____

CONVENTIONAL WRITING INDICATORS (continued)

Students' Names

The Writer:

Language Conventions (continued)
- uses apostrophes for contractions
- writes effectively in both first and third person
- uses appropriate subject-verb agreements
- uses appropriate noun-pronoun agreements
- maintains appropriate tense throughout text

Strategies
◆ **uses a range of strategies for planning, revising and publishing own written texts**
- selects relevant information from a variety of sources before writing
- can transfer information from reading to writing, e.g. takes notes for project
- brainstorms to elicit ideas and information before writing
- attempts to organise ideas before writing
- plans writing using notes, lists or diagrams or other relevant information
- sets and monitors goals for writing
- uses knowledge of other texts as models for writing
- re-reads and revises while composing

Attitude
- writes for enjoyment
- writes to get things done
- experiments with calligraphy, graphics and different formats
- manipulates language for fun, e.g. puns, symbolic character or placenames (Ms Chalk, the teacher, Pitsville).

Teacher's Notes:

Dates:

CLASS

PROFICIENT WRITING INDICATORS

Students' Names

The Writer:

Content and Organisation and Contextual Understandings

◆ **selects text forms to suit purpose and audience, demonstrating control over most essential elements**

◆ **can explain the goals in writing a text and indicate the extent to which they were achieved**

◆ **writes to define, clarify and develop ideas and express creativity, e.g. stories, poems, reports, arguments**

◆ **writes a topic sentence and includes relevant information to develop a cohesive paragraph**

◆ **organises paragraphs logically to form a cohesive text**

◆ **uses a variety of simple, compound and complex sentences appropriate to text form**

• identifies likely audiences and adjusts writing to achieve impact

• conveys a sense of personal involvement in imaginative writing

• conducts research effectively in order to select appropriate information to fulfil task demands

• demonstrates success in writing a wide range of forms, e.g. stories, reports, expository texts, poems, plays

• has sufficient quality ideas to fulfil task demands

• develops topic fully

• uses a plan to organise ideas

• sustains coherence and cohesion throughout text

• demonstrates ability to view writing from a reader's perspective

• expresses a well-reasoned point of view in writing

• can justify a decision in writing

• can write about the same topic from different points of view

• writes a complete, succinct orientation and develops relevant ideas and events

• uses complex sentences with embedded clauses or phrases, e.g. 'My friend Jane, who lives next door, ...'

continued on next page

Teacher's Notes:

Dates:

CLASS _____

PROFICIENT WRITING INDICATORS (continued)

Students' Names

The Writer:

Content and Organisation and Contextual Understandings (continued)

- discusses and uses a range of linking words, e.g. thus, furthermore, in addition
- signals cause and effect using *if, then, because, so, since, result in, brings about, hence, consequently, subsequently*
- signals comparisons using *like, different from, however, resembles, whereas, similar*
- signals alternatives using *on the other hand, otherwise, conversely, either, instead (of), whether*
- signals time order using *later, meanwhile, subsequently, initially, finally*

Word Usage

- ◆ **uses a wide range of words that clearly and precisely convey meaning in a particular form**
- discusses selection of words, clauses or phrases for their shades of meaning and impact on style
- chooses appropriate words to create atmosphere and mood
- elaborates ideas to convey coherent meaning
- sustains appropriate language throughout, e.g. formal language in a business letter
- uses humour, sarcasm or irony
- uses idioms and colloquialisms to enhance writing
- attempts to involve the reader by the use of metaphor, simile, imagery and other literary devices that require commitment from the reader

Editing

- ◆ **edits own writing during and after composing**
- attempts to re-order words, phrases, clauses and paragraphs to clarify and achieve precise meaning
- uses a revising and editing checklist to improve own writing.

continued on next page

Teacher's Notes:

Dates:

CLASS

PROFICIENT WRITING INDICATORS (continued)

Student's' Names

The Writer:

Language Conventions

◆ **demonstrates accurate use of punctuation**

- demonstrates accurate use of:

  capital letters

  full stops

  commas for a variety of purposes

  quotation marks

  exclamation marks

  apostrophes for contractions

  apostrophes for ownership

  paragraphing

  brackets and dashes

- uses punctuation to enhance meaning

Strategies

◆ **takes notes, selects and synthesises relevant information and plans text sequence**

- evaluates writing of others

Attitude

- writes for enjoyment, to get things done and for personal expression

- shows interest in the craft of writing

- is resourceful in gathering information.

Teacher's Notes:

Dates:

CLASS

ADVANCED WRITING INDICATORS

Students' Names

The Writer:

Content, Organisation and Contextual Understandings

◆ controls effectively the language and structural features of a large repertoire of text forms

◆ controls and manipulates the linguistic and structural components of writing to enhance clarity and impact

◆ generates, explores and develops topics and ideas

◆ may choose to manipulate or abandon conventional text forms to achieve impact

◆ maintains stylistic features throughout texts

◆ makes critical choices of tone and point of view to suit different purposes and to influence audiences

◆ writes exploring and developing abstract ideas

◆ makes informed choices about the linguistic features, organisation and development of ideas and information according to audience and purpose

◆ deliberately structures sentences to enhance a text and according to audience and purpose

◆ develops ideas and information clearly, sustaining coherence throughout complex texts

◆ conceals personal bias where appropriate

Word Usage

◆ selects and manipulates words, phrases or clauses, for their shades of meaning and impact

◆ successfully involves the reader by the use of literary devices such as metaphor, simile, onomatopoeia

◆ uses abstract and technical terms appropriately in context.

continued on next page
Teacher's Notes:

Dates:

CLASS _____

ADVANCED WRITING INDICATORS (continued)

Students' Names

The Writer:

Editing

◆ modifies and restructures phrases, clauses, paragraphs or whole texts to clarify and achieve precise meaning

Language Conventions

◆ controls the conventions of writing but may make a deliberate choice to break them to enhance meaning

Strategies

◆ takes responsibility for planning, revising and proof reading to ensure that writing achieves its purpose

◆ reflects on, and critically evaluates own writing to ensure that content and organisation suit the purpose for writing and the audience

◆ evaluates and synthesises information from a variety of sources to support view

Attitude

◆ responds to a compulsion to write

◆ reflects on, critically evaluates and critiques own writing and that of others.

Teacher's Notes:

Dates:

Whole Class Profile Sheets
Key Indicators Only

The whole class profile sheets key indicators only show all key indicators from the first four Writing Developmental Continuum phases. The fifth phase (Independent) is shown on a separate page as all indicators in this phase are key indicators.

Why use the Key Indicator Sheets?

The key indicators can be used by teachers to quickly ascertain children's stage of writing development and get an accurate class profile. The information can be used by teachers to plan future teaching and allocate resources appropriately.

How to use the Key Indicator Profile Sheets?

- Collect samples of writing
- Observe children's writing behaviours
- Highlight indicators observed
- Write entry date and highlighter colour used

When would you use Indicator Profile Sheets?

Teachers may use these sheets to get a quick profile of a new class or to help when reporting to parents. Schools may decide on set times (say twice each year) for this information to be collected and analysed.

CLASS _____

Students' Names

KEY INDICATORS

PHASE 1: Role Play Writing

The Writer:

Content, Organisation and Contextual Understandings

◆ assigns a message to own symbols

◆ understands that writing and drawing are different, e.g. points to words while 'reading'

◆ is aware that print carries a message

Concepts and Conventions

◆ uses known letters or approximations of letters to represent written language

◆ shows beginning awareness of directionality; i.e. points to where print begins.

PHASE 2: Experimental Writing

The Writer:

Content, Organisation and Contextual Understandings

◆ reads back own writing

◆ attempts familiar forms of writing, e.g. lists, letters, recounts, stories, messages

◆ writes using simplified oral language structures, e.g. 'I brt loles'

◆ uses writing to convey meaning

Concepts and Conventions

◆ realises that print contains a constant message

◆ uses left to right and top to bottom orientation of print

◆ demonstrates one-to-one correspondence between written and spoken words

Strategies

◆ relies heavily on the most obvious sounds of a word.

continued on next page
Teacher's Notes:

Dates:

KEY INDICATORS (continued)

Students' Names

PHASE 3: Early Writing

The Writer:

Content, Organisation and Contextual Understandings

◆ uses a small range of familiar text forms

◆ chooses topics that are personally significant

◆ uses basic sentence structures and varies sentence beginnings

◆ can explain in context, some of the purposes of using writing, e.g. shopping list or telephone messages as a memory aid

Word Usage

◆ experiments with words drawn from language experience activites, literature, media and oral language of peers and others

Editing

◆ begins to develop editing skills

Language Conventions

◆ attempts to use some punctuation

Strategies

◆ talks with others to plan and revise own writing.

PHASE 4: Conventional Writing

The Writer:

Content and Organisation and Contextual Understandings

◆ uses text forms to suit purpose and audience

◆ can explain why some text forms may be more appropriate than others to achieve a specific purpose

◆ writes a range of text forms including stories, reports, procedures and expositions

◆ uses a variety of simple, compound and extended sentences

◆ groups sentences containing related information into paragraphs

continued on next page

Teacher's Notes:

Dates:

CLASS _____

Student' Names

KEY INDICATORS (continued)

PHASE 4: Conventional Writing (continued)

The Writer:

Word Usage

◆ is beginning to select vocabulary according to the demands of audience and purpose, e.g. uses subject-specific vocabulary

Editing

◆ uses proof-reading guide or checklist to edit own or peers' writing

Language Conventions

◆ punctuates simple sentences correctly

Strategies

◆ uses a range of strategies for planning, revising and publishing own written texts.

PHASE 5: Proficient Writing

The Writer:

Content and Organisation and Contextual Understandings

◆ selects text forms to suit purpose and audience, demonstrating control over most essential elements

◆ can explain the goals in writing a text and indicate the extent to which they were achieved

◆ writes to define, clarify and develop ideas and express creativity, e.g. stories, poems, reports, arguments

◆ writes a topic sentence and includes relevant information to develop a cohesive paragraph

◆ organises paragraphs logically to form a cohesive text

◆ uses a variety of simple, compound and complex sentences appropriate to text form

Word Usage

◆ uses a wide range of words that clearly and precisely convey meaning in a particular form

continued on next page
Teacher's Notes:

Dates:

Whole Class Profile Sheet Key Indicators Only

Students' Names

KEY INDICATORS (continued)

PHASE 5: Proficient Writing (continued)

The Writer:

Editing

◆ edits own writing during and after composing

Language Conventions

◆ demonstrates accurate use of punctuation

Strategies

◆ takes notes, selects and synthesises relevant information and plans text sequence.

PHASE 6: Advanced Writing

The Writer:

Content, Organisation and Contextual Understandings

◆ controls effectively the language and structural features of a large repertoire of text forms

◆ controls and manipulates the linguistic and structural components of writing to enhance clarity and impact

◆ generates, explores and develops topics and ideas

◆ may choose to manipulate or abandon conventional text forms to achieve impact

◆ maintains stylistic features throughout texts

◆ makes critical choices of tone and point of view to suit different purposes and to influence audiences

◆ writes exploring and developing abstract ideas

◆ makes informed choices about the linguistic features, organisation and development of ideas and information according to audience and purpose

◆ deliberately structures sentences to enhance a text and according to audience and purpose

◆ develops ideas and information clearly, sustaining coherence throughout complex texts

◆ conceals personal bias where appropriate.

continued on next page

Teacher's Notes:

Dates:

CLASS _____

KEY INDICATORS (continued)

PHASE 6: Advanced Writing (continued)

The Writer:

Word Usage

◆ selects and manipulates words, phrases or clauses, for their shades of meaning and impact

◆ successfully involves the reader by the use of literary devices such as metaphor, simile, onomatopoeia

◆ uses abstract and technical terms appropriately in context

Editing

◆ modifies and restructures phrases, clauses, paragraphs or whole texts to clarify and achieve precise meaning

Language Conventions

◆ controls the conventions of writing but may make a deliberate choice to break them to enhance meaning

Strategies

◆ takes responsibility for planning, revising and proof reading to ensure that writing achieves its purpose

◆ reflects on, and critically evaluates own writing to ensure that content and organisation suit the purpose for writing and the audience

◆ evaluates and synthesises information from a variety of sources to support view

Attitude

◆ responds to a compulsion to write

◆ reflects on, critically evaluates and critiques own writing and that of others.

Teacher's Notes:

Dates:

Acknowledgements

The First Steps Developmental Continua were written by the FIRST STEPS TEAM under the direction of Alison Dewsbury.

The Writing Developmental Continuum was written by Glenda Raison, Education Officer, First Steps Project, Education Department of Western Australia, in collaboration with Judith Rivalland, Lecturer in Communications Education, Edith Cowan University.

We gratefully acknowledge the work of :
Dr Peter Sloan and Dr Ross Latham, Edith Cowan University, Perth, Western Australia
Terry D. Johnson, Professor of Education, Faculty of Education, University of Victoria, British Columbia, Canada
Kay Kovalevs for her dedication and hard work in the editing and coordination of the First Steps books in the early years of the project.
Ross Bindon
Caroline Barratt-Pugh for her contribution on working with children for whom English is a second language.

The First Steps project acknowledges the invaluable contributions made by the schools and teachers listed below and by all the school principals who have supported their staffs as they participated in the First Steps Project:
- Challis Early Childhood Education Centre
- Grovelands Early Childhood Education Centre
- Tuart Hill Junior Primary School
- Glen Forrest Primary School
were involved in action research that focused on the use of different Continua.

The Project received a great deal of assistance from the following Primary Schools:
- Carey Park Primary School
- Hollywood Primary School
- Medina Primary School
- Midvale Primary School
- Mingenew Primary School
- West Busselton Primary School
- Wilson Primary School
- Kalgoorlie Central Primary School
- Boulder Primary School
- Boulder Junior Primary School.

The Project is also grateful to **Wagin District High School** in the Narrogin District and the schools in the Esperance District — the **Bremer Bay, Castletown, Condingup, Esperance, Fitzgerald, Gairdner, Grass Patch, Jerdacuttup, Lake King, Munglinup, Nulsen, Ongerup** and **Varley Primary Schools**, which, with **Jerramungup** and **Ravensthorpe District High Schools**, achieved so much in an associate role between 1989 and 1991. These schools provided examples of exemplary practice and documentation that enabled the Project team to refine and extend aspects of First Steps.

The Gosnells Oral Language Project was initiated by **Wirrabirra Education Support Unit** and **Ashburton Drive, Gosnells, Huntingdale, Seaforth** and **Wirrabirra Primary Schools** under the leadership of **Leanne Allen** and **Judith Smailes**. First Steps supported this project with funding, editorial and publishing assistance.

First Steps and Aboriginal Children

Warakurna, Wingellina and **Blackstone Schools** took part in the **Ngaanyatjarra Lands Project** coordinated by **Sandi Percival**. Action research was carried out in these schools, evaluating the use of the First Steps Developmental Continua and related materials with children from the Central Desert.

Fitzroy Crossing District High School, Gogo and **Wangkajungka Primary Schools** participated in a special project designed to adapt the Continua and strategies to the needs of children in Kimberley schools. **Margi Webb** and **Chris Street** worked with colleagues to accomplish this task.

The following schools also addressed the literacy learning of Aboriginal students as part of a special project: in the Narrogin District, **Narrogin Primary School** and **Pingelly** and **Wagin District High Schools**; in the **Kalgoorlie District, Menzies Primary School** and **Laverton** and **Leonora District High Schools** in the **Karratha District,**

Roebourne and Onslow Primary Schools; in the Kimberley District, Dawul and Jungdranung Primary Schools and Kununurra District High School; and in the Bayswater District, Midvale Primary School.

First Steps and Children for Whom English is a Second Language

The Highgate Primary School, with its Intensive Language Centre, has undertaken a special project designed to ensure that First Steps meets the needs of children for whom English is a second or foreign language. Anna Sinclair was the coordinator of this Project. Kay Kovalevs also contributed to and collated the ESL research into children's language learning at Christmas Island District High School.

Finally, special thanks must go to the children who have contributed their writing.

References

Cambourne, B. 1988, *The Whole Story – Natural Learning and the Acquisition of Literacy in the Classroom,* Ashton Scholastic, Sidney.

Chall, J. 1984, *Stages of Reading Development,* McGraw Hill, New York, USA.

Curtan University of Technology 1988, *Language In-Service Course (LINC),* Ministry of Education, Perth.

Education Department of South Australia 1978, *Resource Book of the Development of Reading Skills,* Carroll's Educational Publications, Adelaide.

Education Department of Tasmania 1988, *Pathways of Language Development,* Education Department of Tasmania, Hobart.

Education Department of Western Australia 1987, *Reading to Learn in the Secondary School,* Education Department of Western Australia, Perth

Education Department of Western Australia 1988, *Management and Resources in the Early Years,* Education Department of Western Australia, Perth

Glazer, S. Searfoss, L. and Gentile, L. (Eds) 1988, *Reading Diagnosis New Trends and Procedures,* International Reading Association, Delaware, USA

Graves, D. 1994, A *Fresh Look at Writing,* Heinemann, Portsmouth, NH, USA.

Harwayne, S. 2001, *Writing Through Childhood, Rethinking Process and Product,* Heinemann, Portsmouth, NH, USA

Holdaway, D. 1972, *Independence in Reading. A Handbook on Individualized Procedures,* Ashton Scholastic, Auckland, NZ

Kemp, M. 1987, *Watching Children Read and Write Observational Records for Children with Special Needs,* Nelson, Melbourne

Mason, J. and Au, K. 1986, *Reading Instruction for Today,* Scott, Foresman & Co., Glenview, IL, USA

McCarrier, A., Pinnell, G. S. and Fountas, I. R. 2000, *Interactive Writing: How Language and Literacy Come Together, K-2.* Portsmouth, NH, USA

McCracken, M.J. and R.A. 1979, *Reading Writing & Language A Practical Guide for Primary Teachers,* Pequis Publishers, Winnipeg, Canada

Heller, M.F, *Reading and Writing Connections,* 2nd ed., 1999, Lawrence Erlbaum Associates, Mahawah, New Jersey USA

Ray, K. W. 1999, *Wondrous Words: Writers and Writing in the Elementary Classroom,* National Council of Teachers of English, Urbana, IL, USA

Sloan, P. and Latham, R. 1981, Teaching *Reading IS,* Thomas Nelson, Melbourne

Strunk, William and White, E. B. 2000, *The Elements of Style*, 3rd edition, MacMillan, New York

Thomson, J. 1987, *Understanding Teenagers' Reading and Writing Processes and the Teaching of Literature,* Methuen, North Ryde NSW

Tompkins, G. E. 2001, *Language Arts: Content and Teaching Strategies,* 5th ed., Prentice-Hall, Upper Saddle River, NJ, USA

Weaver, C. 2003, *Reading Process and Practice*, 3rd ed. Heinemann, Portsmouth, NH, USA

evelopmental Continuum

ing that the child is exhibiting all the key indicators of that phase.
dren will also display indicators from other phases

Student's Name _____

I. D. _____

School _____

PHASE 6: Advanced Writing

- signals time order using *later, meanwhile, subsequently, initially, finally*

Word Usage

- ◆ **uses a wide range of words that clearly and precisely convey meaning in a particular form**

- discusses selection of words, clauses or phrases for their shades of meaning and impact on style

- chooses appropriate words to create atmosphere and mood

- elaborates ideas to convey coherent meaning

- sustains appropriate language throughout, e.g. formal language in a business letter

- uses humour, sarcasm or irony

- uses idioms and colloquialisms to enhance writing

- attempts to involve the reader by the use of metaphor, simile, imagery and other literary devices that require commitment from the reader

Editing

- ◆ **edits own writing during and after composing**

- attemps to re-order words, phrases, clauses and paragraphs to clarify and achieve precise meaning

- uses a revising and editing checklist to improve own writing

Language Conventions

- ◆ **demonstrates accurate use of punctuation**

- demonstrates accurate use of:
  capital letters
  full stops
  commas for a variety of purposes
  quotation marks
  exclamation marks
  apostrophes for contractions
  apostrophes for ownership
  paragraphing
  brackets and dashes

- uses punctuation to enhance meaning

Strategies

- ◆ **takes notes, selects and synthesises relevant information and plans text sequence.**

- evaluates writing of others

Attitude

- writes for enjoyment, to get things done and for personal expression

- shows interest in the craft of writing

- is resourceful in gathering information

Content, Organisation and Contextual Understandings

- ◆ **controls effectively the language and structural features of a large repertoire of text forms**

- ◆ **controls and manipulates the linguistic and structural components of writing to enhance clarity and impact**

- ◆ **generates, explores and develops topics and ideas**

- ◆ **may choose to manipulate or abandon conventional text forms to achieve impact**

- ◆ **maintains stylistic features throughout texts**

- ◆ **makes critical choices of tone and point of view to suit different purposes and to influence audiences**

- ◆ **writes exploring and developing abstract ideas**

- ◆ **makes informed choices about the linguistic features, organisation and development of ideas and information according to audience and purpose**

- ◆ **deliberately structures sentences to enhance a text and according to audience and purpose**

- ◆ **develops ideas and information clearly, sustaining coherence throughout complex texts**

- ◆ **conceals personal bias where appropriate**

Word Usage

- ◆ **selects and manipulates words, phrases or clauses, for their shades of meaning and impact**

- ◆ **successfully involved the reader by the use of literary devices such as metaphor, simile, onomatopoeia**

- ◆ **uses abstract and technical terms appropriately in context**

Editing

- ◆ **modifies and restructures phrases, clauses, paragraphs or whole texts to clarify and achieve precise meaning**

Language Conventions

- ◆ **controls the conventions of writing but may make a deliberate choice to break them to enhance meaning.**

Strategies

- ◆ **takes responsibility for planning, revising and proof reading to ensure that writing achieves its purpose**

- ◆ **reflects on, and critically evaluates own writing to ensure that content and organisation suit the purpose for writing and the audience**

- ◆ **evaluates and synthesises information from a variety of sources to support view.**

Attitude

- ◆ **responds to a compulsion to write**

- ◆ **reflects on, critically evaluates and critiques own writing and that of others**

Year: _____ Teacher: _____

Year: _____ Teacher: _____

Year: _____ Teacher: _____

Year: _____ Teacher: _____

Year: _____ Teacher: _____

Year: _____ Teacher: _____

Year: _____ Teacher: _____

Year: _____ Teacher: _____

Phases

PHASE 1: Role Play Writing

Content, Organisation and Contextual Understandings

- ◆ **assigns a message to own symbols**
- ◆ **understands that writing and drawing are different, e.g. points to words while 'reading'**
- ◆ **is aware that print carries a message**
- orally recounts own experiences
- knows some favourite parts of stories, rhymes, jingles or songs
- reads text from memory or invents meaning (the meaning may change each time)
- writes and asks others to assign meaning to what has been written
- talks about own drawing and writing
- tells adults what to write, e.g.' This is my cat'
- role plays writing message for purpose, e.g. telephone messages
- states purpose for own 'writing', e.g. 'This is my shopping list'
- recognises own name (or part of it) in print, e.g. 'My name starts with that'
- attempts to write own name
- thinks own 'writing' can be read by others

Concepts and Conventions

- ◆ **uses known letters or approximations of letters to represent written language**
- ◆ **shows beginning awareness of directionality; i.e. points to where print begins**
- draws symbols consisting of straight, curved or intersecting lines that simulate letters
- makes random marks on paper
- produces aimless or circular scribble
- makes horizontal or linear scribble with some breaks
- places letters randomly on page
- writes random strings of letters
- mixes letters, numerals and invented letter shapes
- flips or reverses letters
- makes organisational decisions about writing, e.g. 'I'll start here so it will fit'
- copies layout of some text forms, e.g. letters, lists

Strategies

- experiments with upper and lower case letters. May show a preference for upper case
- repeats a few known alphabet symbols frequently using letters from own name
- copies print from environment

Attitude

- enjoys stories and asks for them to be retold or reread
- listens attentively to the telling or reading of stories and other texts
- 'writes' spontaneously for self rather than for an audience

PHASE 2: Experimental Writing

Content, Organisation and Contextual Understandings

- ◆ **reads back own writing**
- ◆ **attempts familiar forms of writing, e.g. lists, letters, recounts, stories, messages**
- ◆ **writes using simplified oral language structures, e.g. 'I brt loles'**
- ◆ **uses writing to convey meaning**
- voices thoughts while writing
- writes to communicate messages, direct experiences or feelings
- assumes that reader shares the context so may not give sufficient background information, e.g. may tell 'who' but not 'when'
- often begins sentence with 'I' or 'We'
- is beginning to use written language structures. Has a sense of sentence, i.e. writes complete sentences with or without punctuation
- repeats familiar words when writing, e.g. cat, cat, cat
- generates writing by repeating the same beginning patterns, e.g. 'I like cats, I like dogs, I like birds ...'
- recognises some words and letters in context
- recognises that people use writing to convey meaning

Concepts and Conventions

- ◆ **realises that print contains a constant message**
- ◆ **uses left to right and top to bottom orientation of print**
- ◆ **demonstrates one-to-one correspondence between written and spoken word**
- uses upper and lower case letters indiscriminately
- distinguishes between numerals and letters
- leaves a space between word-like clusters of letters
- dictates slowly so teacher can 'keep up' while scribing

Year: _____ **Teacher:** _____   **Year:** _____ **Teacher:** _____   **Year:** _____ **Teacher:** _____

Year: _____ **Teacher:** _____   **Year:** _____ **Teacher:** _____   **Year:** _____ **Teacher:** _____

Developmental Continuum

rving that the child is exhibiting all the key indicators of that phase.
dren will also display indicators from other phases

Student's Name _____

I. D. _____

School _____

PHASE 3: Early Writing

Strategies

- ◆ **relies heavily on the most obvious sounds of a word**
- tells others what has been written
- asks others what has been written
- traces and copies letters with some successful formations
- points to 'words' while reading own writing
- voices thoughts while writing
- reads back what has been written to clarify meaning
- experiments with, and over-generalises, print conventions, e.g. puts a full stop after each word
- uses knowledge of rhyme to spell words written
- uses print resources in classroom, e.g. charts, signs, word banks

Attitude

- listens attentively to the telling or reading of stories and other texts
- writes spontaneously for self or chosen audience

Content, Organisation and Contextual Understandings

- ◆ **uses a small range of familiar text forms**
- ◆ **chooses topics that are personally significant**
- ◆ **uses basic sentence structures and varies sentence beginnings**
- ◆ **can explain in context, some of the purposes of using writing, e.g. shopping list or telephone messages as a memory aid**
- uses a partial organisational framework, e.g. simple orientation and story development
- often writes a simple recount of personal events or observation and comment
- uses time order to sequence and organise writing
- is beginning to use some narrative structure
- is beginning to use some informational text structures, e.g. recipes, factual description
- writes simple factual accounts with little elaboration
- includes irrelevant detail in 'dawn-to-dark' recounts
- attempts to orient, or create a context for the reader, but may assume a shared context
- rewrites known stories in sequence
- includes detail in written retell
- includes several items of information about a topic
- is beginning to use 'book' language, e.g. 'By the fire sat a cat'.
- joins simple sentences (often overusing the same connectors, e.g. 'and', 'then')
- uses knowledge of rhyme, rhythm and repetition in writing
- repeats familiar patterns, e.g. 'In the jungle I saw ...'

Word Usage

- ◆ **experiments with words drawn from language experience activites, literature, media and oral language of peers and others**
- discusses word formations and meanings; noticing similarities and differences
- transfers words encountered in talk, or reading, to writing
- highlights words for emphasis, e.g. BIG

Editing

- ◆ **begins to develop editing skills**
- deletes words to clarify meaning
- adds words to clarify meaning
- begins to proofread for spelling errors
- responds to requests for clarification
- attempts the use of a proofreading guide constructed jointly by students and teacher

Language Conventions

- ◆ **attempts to use some punctuation**
- sometimes uses full stops
- sometimes uses a capital letter to start a sentence
- uses capital letters for names
- attempts use of question marks
- attempts use of exclamation marks
- sometimes uses apostrophes for contractions
- overgeneralises use of print conventions, e.g. overuse of apostrophes, full stops, dashes and commas
- often writes in the first person
- attempts writing in both first and third person
- usually uses appropriate subject/verb agreements
- usually maintains consistent tense
- writes a title which reflects content

Strategies

- ◆ **talks with others to plan and revise own writing**
- re-reads own writing to maintain word sequence
- attempts to transfer knowledge of text structure to writing, e.g. imitates form of a familiar big book
- shares ideas for writing with peers or teacher
- participates in group brainstorming activities to elicit ideas and information before writing
- in consultation with teacher, sets personal goals for writing development
- discusses proofreading strategies with peers and teacher and attemps to use them in context

Attitude

- perseveres to complete writing tasks

Year: _____ **Teacher:** _____

Year: _____ **Teacher:** _____

Phases

PHASE 4: Conventional Writing

Content and Organisation and Contextual Understandings

- ◆ **uses text forms to suit purpose and audience**
- ◆ **can explain why some text forms may be more appropriate than others to achieve a specific purpose**
- ◆ **writes a range of text forms including stories, reports, procedures and expositions**
- ◆ **uses a variety of simple, compound and extended sentences**
- ◆ **groups sentences containing related information into paragraphs**

- takes account of some aspects of context, purpose and audience
- considers the needs of audience and includes background information
- uses rhyme, rhythm and repetition for effect (where appropriate)
- demonstrates the ability to develop a topic
- demonstrates knowledge of differences between narrative and informational text when writing
- organises the structure of writing more effectively, e.g. uses headings, subheadings
- can write from another's point of view
- shows evidence of personal voice (where appropriate)
- is developing a personal style of writing
- establishes place, time and situation
- often includes dialogue
- uses dialogue to enhance character development
- shows evidence of the transfer of literary language from reading to writing
- organises paragraphs logically
- uses titles and headings appropriately
- orders ideas in time order or other sequence such as priority order
- uses a variety of linking words such as *and, so, because, if, next, after, before, first.*

Word Usage

- ◆ **is beginning to select vocabulary according to the demands of audience and purpose, e.g. uses subject-specific vocabulary**

- uses some similes or metaphors in an attempt to enhance meaning
- varies vocabulary for interest
- includes specific vocabulary to explain or describe, e.g. appropriate adjectives
- uses adverbs and adjectives to enhance meaning
- uses simple colloquialisms and clichés

Editing

- ◆ **uses proofreading guide or checklist to edit own or peers' writing**
- edits and proofreads own writing after composing
- reorders text to clarify meaning, e.g. moves words, phrases and clauses
- reorders words to clarify meaning
- attempts to correct punctuation
- recognises most misspelled words and attempts corrections

Language Conventions

- ◆ **punctuates simple sentences correctly**
- uses capital letters for proper nouns
- uses capital letters to start sentences
- uses capital letters for titles
- uses full stops to end sentences
- uses question marks correctly
- sometimes uses commas
- uses apostrophes for possession
- writes apostrophes for contractions
- writes effectively in both first and third person
- uses appropriate subject-verb agreements
- uses appropriate noun-pronoun agreements
- maintains appropriate tense throughout text

Strategies

- ◆ **uses a range of strategies for planning, revising and publishing own written texts**
- selects relevant information from a variety of sources before writing
- can transfer information from reading to writing, e.g. takes notes for project
- brainstorms to elicit ideas and information before writing
- attempts to organise ideas before writing
- plans writing using notes, lists or diagrams or other relevant information
- sets and monitors goals for writing
- uses knowledge of other texts as models for writing
- rereads and revises while composing

Attitude

- writes for enjoyment
- writes to get things done
- experiments with calligraphy, graphics and different formats
- manipulates language for fun, e.g. puns, symbolic character or placenames (Ms Chalk, the teacher, Pitsville)

PHASE 5: Proficient Writing

Content, Organisation and Contextual Understandings

- ◆ **selects text forms to suit purpose and audience, demonstrating control over most essential elements**
- ◆ **can explain the goals in writing a text and indicate the extent to which they were achieved**
- ◆ **writes to define, clarify and develop ideas and express creativity, e.g. stories, poems, reports, arguments**
- ◆ **writes a topic sentence and includes relevant information to develop a cohesive paragraph**
- ◆ **organises paragraphs logically to form a cohesive text**
- ◆ **uses a variety of simple, compound and complex sentences appropriate to text form**

- identifies likely audiences and adjusts writing to achieve impact
- conveys a sense of personal involvement in imaginative writing
- conducts research effectively in order to select appropriate information to fulfil task demands
- demonstrates success in writing a wide range of forms, e.g. stories, reports, expository texts, poems, plays
- has sufficient quality ideas to fulfil task demands
- develops topic fully
- uses a plan to organise ideas
- sustains coherence and cohesion throughout text
- demonstrates ability to view writing from a reader's perspective
- expresses a well reasoned point of view in writing
- can justify a decision in writing
- can write about the same topic from different points of view
- writes a complete, succinct orientation and develops relevant ideas and events
- uses complex sentences with embedded clauses or phrases, e.g. 'My friend Jane, who lives next door, ...'
- discusses and uses a range of linking words, e.g. thus, furthermore, in addition
- signals cause and effect using *if, then, because, so, since, result in, brings about, hence, consequently, subsequently*
- signals comparisons using *like, different from, however, resembles, whereas, similar*
- signals alternatives using *on the other hand, otherwise, conversely, either, instead (of), whether*

g that the child is exhibiting all the key indicators of that phase.
will also display indicators from other phases

g	PHASE 4: Conventional Writing	PHASE 5: Proficient Writing
are personally significant. They needs. They have a sense of eal with one or two elements of ut not punctuation.	Writers are familiar with most aspects of the writing process and are able to select forms to suit different purposes. Their control of structure, punctuation and spelling may vary according to the complexity of the writing task.	Writers have developed a personal style of writing and are able to manipulate forms of writing to suit their purposes. They have control over spelling and punctuation. They choose from a large vocabulary and their writing is cohesive, coherent and satisfying.

Handwriting samples

15/5/89
was a fiery dinosaur and one uras Recks came en and Big e Tyrannasaurs the dinosaurs. ever after Nathan.

The First Boomerang
One day, manny years ago, there lived an aboriginal carpenter named Kesaw. He was well respected by his tribe and was noted for his creative sculptures. For many years he had carved creatures from the local jarrah trees.
As he sat in the warm spring sun a sleepy snake slithered by. Kesaw decided to carve a snake. Slowly he got up to find the right piece of wood. When he was satisfied with his selection he began to whittle away with his best blade. The wood was hard and the carving slow. Kesaw began to get drowsy his head nodded and he fell asleep.

Our heritage
Many of the people who want to save the tree, talk of history and heritage. The tree was a meeting place, a place of happiness, a source of shade on burning summer days after a refreshing swim in the nearly river. But then the traffic built up the river became a murky passage of sludge. The children grew up and had their own children but their children knew nothing of this once peaceful place.

The Writer:

	The Writer:	The Writer:
xt forms ly significant nd varies sentence the purposes of using ephone messages as a from language experience oral language of peers and on vise own writing	◆ uses text forms to suit purpose and audience ◆ can explain why some text forms may be more appropriate than others to achieve a specific purpose ◆ writes a range of text forms including stories, reports, procedures and expositions ◆ uses a variety of simple, compound and extended sentences ◆ groups sentences containing related information into paragraphs ◆ is beginning to select vocabulary according to the demands of audience and purpose, e.g. uses subject-specific vocabulary ◆ uses proof-reading guide or checklist to edit own or peers' writing ◆ punctuates simple sentences correctly ◆ uses a range of strategies for planning, revising and publishing own written texts	◆ selects text forms to suit purpose and audience, demonstrating control over most essential elements ◆ can explain the goals in writing a text and indicate the extent to which they were achieved ◆ writes to define, clarify and develop ideas and express creativity, e.g. stories, poems, reports, arguments ◆ writes a topic sentence and includes relevant information to develop a cohesive paragraph ◆ organises paragraphs logically to form a cohesive text ◆ uses a variety of simple, compound and complex sentences appropriate to text form ◆ uses a wide range of words that clearly and precisely convey meaning in a particular form ◆ edits own writing during and after composing ◆ demonstrates accurate use of punctuation ◆ takes notes, selects and synthesises relevant information and plans text sequence.

Major Teaching Emphases:

hases:	Major Teaching Emphases:	Major Teaching Emphases:
ting is purposeful ween oral and written e of different forms of and audiences rategies d to form a cohesive ed to form a whole text spell new words lop word banks using to enhance meaning inking words de and encourage	◆ teach children to plan and write both narrative and informational texts ◆ help children to adapt their writing to suit the intended purpose and to explore alternative ways of expressing ideas ◆ discuss linguistic features of basic text types ◆ teach children appropriate use of organisational markers such as topic sentences, paragraphs and headings ◆ show different ways of linking paragraphs to form a whole text ◆ encourage the use of a variety of linking words ◆ encourage children to take responsibility for their own learning ◆ teach revising, editing and proof-reading skills ◆ discuss and foster 'personal voice' and individual style in writing ◆ teach children the conventions of language (punctuation, grammar and spelling) in context	◆ provide opportunities for students to analyse, evaluate and structure an extensive variety of forms of text, both narrative and informational ◆ discuss the specific effect of context, audience and purpose on written texts ◆ extend students' knowledge of correct use of writing conventions ◆ teach students to analyse mass media ◆ discuss and foster a sense of 'personal voice', e.g. individual style, tone, rhythm, vocabulary ◆ extend the students' range of planning and revision strategies ◆ encourage students to use writing to reflect on and monitor their own learning ◆ encourage students to read as writers and write as readers

PHASE 6: Advanced Writing not included on this overview

Teachers can identify a child's phase of development by observin
It should be noted however, that most childrer

Phases

PHASE 1: Role Play Writing
Children are beginning to come to terms with a new aspect of language, that of written symbols. They experiment with marks on paper with the intention of communicating a message or emulating adult writing.

PHASE 2: Experimental Writing
Children are aware that speech can be written down and that written messages remain constant. They understand the left to right organisation of print and experiment with writing letters and words.

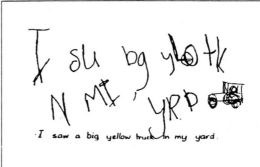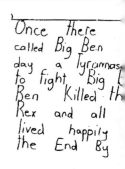

PHASE 3: Early Writi
Children write about topics which are beginning to consider audienc sentence but may only be able to writing at one time, e.g. spelling b

---

Key Indicators

The Writer:
- assigns a message to own symbols
- understands that writing and drawing are different, e.g. points to words while 'reading'
- is aware that print carries a message
- uses known letters or approximations of letters to represent written language
- shows beginning awareness of directionality; i.e. points to where print begins

The Writer:
- reads back own writing
- attempts familiar forms of writing, e.g. lists, letters, recounts, stories, messages
- writes using simplified oral language structures, e.g. 'I brt loles'
- uses writing to convey meaning
- realises that print contains a constant message
- uses left to right and top to bottom orientation of print
- demonstrates one-to-one correspondence between written and spoken word
- relies heavily on the most obvious sounds of a word

The Writer:
- uses a small range of familiar te
- chooses topics that are persona
- uses basic sentence structures a beginnings
- can explain in context, some of writing, e.g. shopping list or tel memory aid
- experiments with words drawn activites, literature, media and others
- begins to develop editing skills
- attempts to use some punctuat
- talks with others to plan and re

Major Teaching Emphases:
- demonstrate the connection between oral and written language
- demonstrate that written messages remain constant
- demonstrate that writing communicates a message
- focus on the way print works (print concepts and conventions)
- demonstrate that writing is purposeful and has an intended audience
- use correct terminology for letters, sounds, words
- encourage children to experiment with writing

Major Teaching Emphases:
- model brief, imaginative and factual texts and explain the purpose and intended audience
- help children build lists of high-frequency words from their reading and writing
- demonstrate the one-to-one correspondence of written and spoken words
- discuss how writing can be used to communicate over time and distance
- encourage children to talk about their experiences
- help children understand how written texts are composed in sentences
- help children develop a stable concept of a word
- help children relate written symbols to the sounds they represent
- talk about letters, words and sentences

Major Teaching Emp
- develop an awareness that w
- talk about the differences bet language
- read, write and discuss a rang writing for different purposes
- teach planning and revision st
- show how sentences are linke paragraph
- show how paragraphs are link
- teach strategies for learning t
- continue to help children deve topic or theme words
- discuss the selection of words
- model the use of appropriate
- introduce a proof-reading gui children to use it

At all phases:
- model good English language use
- model writing every day
- encourage students to reflect on their understandings, gradually building a complete picture of written language structures
- ensure that students have opportunities to write for a variety of audiences and purposes
- encourage students to share their writing experiences